BLACK LEADERS
IN SOUTHERN AFRICAN HISTORY

Black Leaders
in Southern African History

EDITED BY

Christopher Saunders

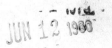

LONDON
HEINEMANN
IBADAN · NAIROBI · LUSAKA

Heinemann Educational Books Ltd
22 Bedford Square, London WC1B 3HH
P.M.B. 5205 Ibadan · P.O. Box 45314 Nairobi
P.O. Box 3966 Lusaka

EDINBURGH   MELBOURNE   AUCKLAND
JOHANNESBURG   HONG KONG   SINGAPORE
KUALA LUMPUR   NEW DELHI   EXETER (NH)
KINGSTON   PORT OF SPAIN

ISBN 0 435 94477 0 (cased)
      0 435 94478 9 (paper)

Photoset in Malta in Lumitype Latine by Interprint Limited
Printed in Great Britain by Biddles Ltd, Guildford, Surrey

Contents

List of Figures and Maps

List of Photographs

Acknowledgements

Photographs: Nos. 1, 2, 9, 13 and 14, Cape Archives; No. 4, University of the Witwatersrand; Nos. 5 and 7 from *Shaka Zulu, The Rise of the Zulu Empire* by E. A. Ritter (Longman, London, 1955, reproduced by permission of Miss Killie Campbell); No. 8, Swaziland National Archives; No. 10 from *The Diamond Mines of South Africa* by Gardner F. Williams (B. F. Buck & Co., 1904); No. 11, Gribble; No. 16 from *Tiyo Soga* by John Chalmers and No. 17, Cory Library, Grahamstown.

Chronological Table

INDIVIDUALS AT AGE ABOUT TWENTY *The names of those discussed in this book are in italics*	EVENTS
1790 Dingiswayo (c.1770–1818)	**1778** Cape Governor demarcates boundary between Cape and Xhosa
1799 *Ngqika* (c.1779–1829)	
1800 Faku (c.1780–1867)	**1779** First Cape-Xhosa war
	1795 First British occupation of the Cape
	1799 War on the Cape eastern frontier
1806 Moshoeshoe (c.1786–1870)	c.**1805** 'Madlathule' famine in Zululand
1807 Shaka (c.1787–1828)	**1806** Second British occupation of the Cape
1810 Hintsa (c.1790–1835)	
1815 *Mzilikazi* (c.1795–1868)	**1812** Xhosa driven east of Fish river by Cape forces
1815 Dingane (c.1795–1840)	
1818 *Mpande* (c.1798–1872)	c.**1818** Beginning of the *Mfecane*
	1818 Battle of Amalinde
	1819 Ndlambe defeated at Grahamstown
1824 Sekonyela (c.1804–1856)	**1823** Battle of Dithakong
1830 Setshele (c.1810–1892)	**1824** White settlement at Port Natal
1830 Sekhukhune (c. 1810–1882)	**1828** Battle of Mbolompo
1831 *Adam Kok III* (1811–1875)	**1829** Maqomo expelled from Kat river
1834 Sarhili (c.1814–1892)	
1840 *Mascpha* (c.1820–1899)	**1834** Cape-Xhosa war
1840 Sandile (c.1820–1878)	**1836** The Great Trek
1846 *Mswati II* (c.1826–1865)	**1838** Dingane attacks Trekkers
1849 *Tiyc Scga* (1829–1871)	**1846** War of the Axe
1852 *Cetshwayc* (c.1832–1884)	**1850** War of Mlanjeni
1853 Lobengula (c.1833–1894)	
1858 Khama III (c. 1838–1923)	**1856** The Cattle-killing
1878 W. B. Rubusana (1858–1936)	**1868** British annexation of Basutoland
1879 *J. T. Jabavu* (1859–1921)	**1880** Gun War; Transkeian rebellion
1888 Dinizulu (c.1868–1913)	**1886** Gold discovered on the Witwatersrand
1891 J. L. Dube (1871–1946)	**1899** Anglo-Boer War
	1906 Bambaatha rebellion
	1912 Formation of the South African Native National Congress

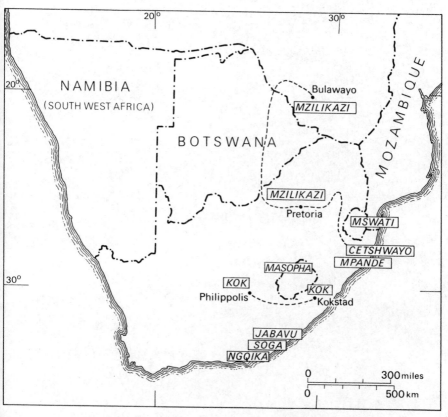

Map of southern Africa: modern boundaries

Introduction

The nine leaders considered in this book are essentially nine-teenth-century figures, though three were born in the eighteenth century and one lived until 1921. A long list might be drawn up of men and women who qualify for inclusion in a collection of essays on black leaders in nineteenth-century southern Africa. Very little is known about the lives of some of those who would appear in such a list; others have been the subject of short bio-graphical sketches in the *Dictionary of South African Biography*, and a few—Shaka and Dingane of the Zulu, or Sandile of the Xhosa, for example—have had full popular biographies devoted to them. Moshoeshoe, founder of the Sotho nation, has perhaps received most attention, two scholarly lives having been pub-lished in 1975. It is not claimed that this book selects for examination the careers of the nine most important blacks in nineteenth-century southern Africa. It does include men whose qualities of leadership differed greatly, and were exercised in very different situations. Some of the nine—such as Mzilikazi or Cetshwayo—are well-known figures, while others—Mpande or Mswati—have suffered undue neglect. All nine were, how-ever, men of stature, whose lives merit attention.

Six of the nine ruled independent states, and Masopha, a son of Moshoeshoe, ruled his section of the southern Sotho with con-siderable independence. Mzilikazi founded his own state, as Shaka had before him. Mpande, Mswati and Adam Kok III each came to office under difficult circumstances, but consolidated his position as ruler and helped maintain his state in the face of serious challenges from within and without. Under Kok the Griqua captaincy gained a new lease of life when it was re-established in new territory, much as Mzilikazi's kingdom had been twenty-five years before. Ngqika, on the other hand, left the western Xhosa divided and weakened. Cetshwayo saw his Zulu kingdom defeated and dismembered.

The response to white intrusion is perhaps the most important theme running through these nine essays. To the young Ngqika the whites posed no serious threat and when the opportunity arose he allied himself with the British, whom he believed could aid him in his struggle for power within the Xhosa polity. This alliance had disastrous results: his people lost much territory and he died a tragic, broken man. It was not until 1836 that whites began to threaten Mzilikazi. The encroachment of the Trekkers on to his lands in the Transvaal, and their readiness to challenge his forces in battle, helped persuade him to move north of the Limpopo river, where he hoped to be out of reach of his various enemies. Mpande came to power in Zululand with the aid of the Trekkers of the Republic of Natalia, and Mswati in turn allied himself with a group of white Transvaalers against Mpande. Cetshwayo's challenge came from the British, who invaded his kingdom in 1879. Sent into exile, he returned to his country hoping to be able to revive his power, only to meet disillusionment and death. The stubborn resistance of Masopha, the arch resister among the southern Sotho, helped force the Cape to hand Lesotho back to the British in the early 1880s, after which he continued to oppose British and Sotho infringements of his independence. Kok sought friendly relations with the British, with whom he signed a treaty in 1843. After being badly treated by them at Philippolis, and then abandoned in 'New Griqualand', he learned with shock in 1874 that his country was to be brought under Cape magisterial rule.

The complex pattern of relations with whites, whether Afrikaners or English, is itself only part of a larger, even more complex reality, which encompasses internecine rivalry and a variety of external challenges. For both Mzilikazi and Mswati, for example, the Zulu, and not the whites, seemed the chief threat. The study of leadership in such situations obviously requires careful attention to a wide variety of sources, and some of the essays in this book draw upon recent, as yet unpublished primary research. In some cases, unfortunately, the sources allow little or no investigation of the personality of the leader involved.

As leaders, Tiyo Soga and John Tengo Jabavu stand apart from the other seven discussed in this book. Both highly gifted men, well-educated in the western tradition, they rose from humble backgrounds to occupy positions of considerable influence among their people. Soga became the first African missionary, while Jabavu's editorship of *Imvo* and his acute political sense helped make him the best-known African in the late nineteenth-century Cape and the leading champion of African rights.

Though Soga, in particular, never forgot his African heritage, both men sought acceptance in elite white society. Their style of leadership, essentially accommodationist, was to be a dominant one—though not the only one—among southern African blacks in the first half of the twentieth century.

White leadership in nineteenth-century South Africa has received a large amount of scholarly attention. Black leadership, the subject of these nine studies, has remained a largely unexplored field. Whereas much recent historical scholarship on southern Africa has concerned itself with the play of material forces and the analysis of changing social structures, a biographical focus can have its own importance in helping to humanize the past and bring it to life, and it forces the historian to consider the difficult question of the role of personality in history. Using such a focus, these essays aim to cast new light on some facets of the nineteenth-century southern African past.

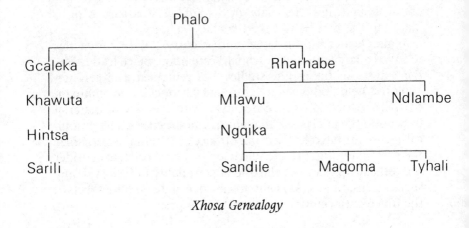

Xhosa Genealogy

1
Ngqika
c.1779–1829

In the late eighteenth and early nineteenth century the
Xhosa polity was rent by internal feuds, as Ngqika com-
peted with Ndlambe and Hintsa for supremacy. At the
same time, the growth of white power on the Fish river
began to pose a serious threat to the western Xhosa.
Ngqika decided to ally himself with the Cape against his
Xhosa enemies—with disastrous results.

Ngqika was probably born in 1779, one year after the first short-
lived agreement between the Xhosa and the Cape Colony and
one year before his grandfather, Rharhabe, made the first friendly
overture to the Boer settlers. When he died fifty years later, the
Xhosa had lost much of their best territory, and were defeated
and divided as never before. Xhosaland lay helpless before the
tide of European settlers, European trade, European religion and
European liquor. Ngqika bears a heavy responsibility for this
transformation, and his name and deeds are a source of some
embarrassment to his descendants and their subjects. Yet he was
a man of considerable intelligence and ability and his ambitions
and methods were certainly no meaner or more reprehensible
than those of his contemporaries. How then did he become a
collaborator?

In essence, the answer is that Ngqika neither understood nor
feared the Europeans until it was too late, and he was caught in
a trap which he had prepared for his enemies. For Ngqika, the
Xhosa world was the only world which mattered, and all his
devices and stratagems were designed and executed with the
intention of placing himself at the head of a strong and centralized Xhosa nation. It is an ironic measure of his miscalculation
that he chose as his ally that power—the Europeans of the Cape
Colony—which turned the dream into an impossibility, whether
for Ngqika or for anyone else.

The Regency of Ndlambe

In 1779 the Xhosa kingdom stretched from the Mbashe river in the east to the Sundays river in the west. It was presided over by the Paramount Chief Khawuta who lived near the centre of his dominion in the neighbourhood of present-day King William's Town. The kingdom was divided into chiefdoms, each ruled by a chief who was a member of the royal clan, that is to say a brother, cousin or uncle of the Paramount. Succession disputes, while not unknown, were at a minimum thanks to the custom whereby each chief's son was encouraged to set up his own chiefdom as soon as he emerged from the circumcision lodge where he had been initiated into manhood. Accompanied by his age-mates, he would colonize new territory subjecting whatever Khoi or non-Xhosa Bantu-speakers he found there. Thus each chief was able to rule his own land and his own subjects without encroaching on the autonomy of any other chief. This benefited the kingdom as a whole in that it enabled it to expand rapidly in all directions, but it undermined the power of the Paramount over his subordinates. The degree of obedience which he commanded varied from chief to chief and from time to time.

Most chiefs preferred to acknowledge the authority of the Paramount, and in return were allowed to govern their chiefdoms with the minimum of interference. But Ngqika's grandfather, Rharhabe (?1725–*c.*1782), was an exception. Rharhabe had challenged his brother Gcaleka for the Paramountcy, and when Gcaleka died, he attacked Gcaleka's heir, Khawuta (1778). Defeated once again, Rharhabe, who was by all accounts a ferocious warrior, turned his attention to the Thembu and died in battle in about 1782. Rharhabe's heir, Mlawu, was killed in the same war, and it was unclear which of Mlawu's two young sons should succeed to the chieftainship of the amaRharhabe (people of Rharhabe). The majority of the councillors chose Ntimbo and sent for the Paramount Khawuta to invest him, but to their surprise he invested Ngqika, who was the choice of Mlawu's younger brother, Ndlambe. By doing this, he indicated his support for Ndlambe, who became ruler of the amaRharhabe as regent for the young Ngqika.

Ndlambe was a shrewd and ambitious man. He wished to build up the power of the amaRharhabe, but he did not repeat

◀ *1 Ngqika*

the mistake of his father, Rharhabe, and attack the Paramount himself. Instead, he concentrated on subduing the other Xhosa chiefs, who, like himself, were autonomous subjects of the Paramount Chief. In this, he was aided by an accident of geography. The amaRharhabe resided west of the Paramount, but they did not lie on the border of Xhosa territory. The chiefs who were the target of Ndlambe's ambitions lay between the amaRharhabe on the one hand and the advancing settler frontier on the other. Rharhabe discovered the strategic possibilities of this situation when he clashed with the imiDange chiefdom in 1779. Temporarily defeated by Rharhabe, the imiDange retreated into Boer territory, only to find themselves embroiled with the Boers, who resented their intrusion. The result was the First Frontier War (1779–81) in which the Boers broke the power of the imiDange. Ndlambe now turned his attention to the powerful amaGqunukhwebe chiefdom. He defeated them three times, driving them deeper and deeper into the Colony, but because they were largely Khoi in composition, they were able to recruit more members among the broken Khoi of the Colony. Eventually, Ndlambe persuaded a small party of Boers to join him in an attack on the amaGqunukhwebe, and with skilful diplomacy, he fomented a war between his various rivals and the Cape Colony. This culminated in the Boer expedition of 1793 (sometimes known as the Second Frontier War), which drove the amaGqunukhwebe, the imiDange and other minor chiefdoms beyond the Fish to the Tsholomnqa river just west of modern King William's Town, where Ndlambe was waiting for them. In the great battle which followed, he scored a crushing victory which made the amaRharhabe supreme in the west.

The balance of power among the Xhosa chiefs had altered drastically as the result of Ndlambe's strategy. The amaRharhabe were no longer merely one of a number of autonomous chiefdoms jointly subject to the Paramount but masters of the whole of western Xhosaland. Meanwhile, the eastern Xhosa chiefdoms were riven with dissensions of their own and Khawuta, who had proved rather a weak Paramount, died leaving his heir, Hintsa, still a boy. The time was now ripe for the amaRharhabe to seize the Paramountcy. It is not clear whether this was Ndlambe's intention but he never had an opportunity, for, shortly after his victory, he was attacked and overthrown by his nephew and ward, Ngqika.

Ngqika in Power

Ngqika's attack on Ndlambe in 1795 came as a surprise to his uncle. After all, it was Ndlambe's intercession with Khawuta which had made Ngqika chief in the first place, and Ndlambe had seen Ngqika educated, circumcised and installed. Ngqika had fought in the war of 1793, where his praisename, 'A! Lwaganda!' meaning 'He who stamps the ground while fighting', was probably won. But he chafed under the restraint placed on him by the superior influence of his uncle among the people. It was the custom for young men just emerged from circumcision to distinguish themselves in some brave action, and his young age-mates urged him on. 'You see, chief,' they said, 'the *Maduna* [big-shot] is running away with your people, for they have become accustomed to him. Go, pretend you are paying him a courtesy visit and then we shall attack him.'[1] Shortly thereafter, Ngqika visited Ndlambe, ostensibly to settle a court case between their subjects. Oxen were slaughtered for the visitors, and a dance was in progress when Ngqika gave the signal to attack. Ndlambe fled to the Paramount's Great Place and appealed for help from the regent who was ruling during Hintsa's minority. The regent sided with Ndlambe and sent a message to Ngqika, asking him why he was wandering around a country not his own.

Ngqika sent back a defiant reply. His opponents divided their forces in two with the aim of attacking him on two sides at once. But the division commanded by Ndlambe's brother, Mnyaluza, attacked a day early, and Ngqika was thus able to deal with each division separately. The forces of the Paramountcy were thrown back well over the Kei to the Jujura river. Ngqika captured Ndlambe and Hintsa, but Hintsa managed to escape. Ngqika was not yet eighteen; he little knew that he had already come as near as he ever would to achieving his ambition.

Neither birth nor custom had endowed Ngqika with a great and powerful chieftainship. By birth he was only a junior chief, and custom had never allotted the Xhosa chiefs extensive powers over their subjects. As we have seen, Ndlambe had built up the power of the amaRharhabe, and Ngqika had added to that power by defeating not only Ndlambe, but the Paramount as well. For a time, he even took to calling himself Paramount Chief of all the Xhosa. But perhaps even more interesting, and certainly more indicative of his ability, were his attempts to increase the power of the chiefs over the commoners.

A chief's council consisted of two components: those councillors who were dependent on his favour and those who commanded followings of their own. The first group consisted of the chief's circumcision-mates and of men selected by him in recognition of their bravery or wisdom. The second group were heads of commoner clans or clan-sections. These commoner clans had once been independent, but with the rise of the Tshawe royal clan, some time before 1600, they had lost their independence and most of them had split up into clan-sections. Nevertheless, the head of each clan-section still continued to command the hereditary loyalty and obedience of his people. As a result, the chief controlled the majority of his subjects only indirectly, and had to rely on the loyalty of his councillors to execute his orders, to collect his tribute and to furnish him with warriors. The chief had no standing army or police, except for the young men (known as the 'milkers of the Great Place') who had come to earn their bridewealth in his service, and these only stayed a few years at the most. Because of this, the chief could not afford to be too dictatorial. He had to heed the advice of his councillors on political and judicial matters, and he had to be generous in redistributing the cattle which he acquired. If the chief displeased the body of his councillors, they could depose him and adopt another, such as a younger brother, as their chief. Individual councillors who were dissatisfied could flee to rival chiefs, who would welcome them if they were accompanied by their followers and their cattle. In those days, land was plentiful and men were relatively few, and each chief wished to add to his supporters.

Ngqika set out to increase his control over these councillors. He took over homesteads whose headships had fallen vacant and, where possible, he deposed councillors and brought their people under his personal rule. He succeeded in reserving the right of passing the death sentence for himself. However, instead of making use of it, he often substituted a fine in cattle, a measure that was far more profitable in building up a following. He forbade private revenge for adultery and substituted a fine, which added to his jurisdiction as well as to his revenue. His objective in all of this was political power rather than personal gratification. This is clear from his abolition of *upundlc*, a custom which permitted the sexual requisitioning of young women by the chief and his retinue, and which provoked much resentment without serving any useful political purpose. All these innovations were opposed by the councillors, but most especially Ngqika's extension of *isizi*, the custom whereby a chief was paid a beast on the death of a subject. Ngqika ruled that when a man died without heirs in the direct line, his cattle should go not to his relatives (and fellow-clansmen) but to the chief. This almost provoked a rebellion but as the other chiefs soon followed Ngqika's lead, the commoners were left with no choice but to comply.

Even more ingenious was Ngqika's introduction of the *ixhiba* or 'grandfather house'. Conflict between the generations surfaced most clearly among the Xhosa on the death of a chief, when the late chief's councillors were superseded by the heir's councillors. This problem was particularly acute in the case of the councillors of Mlawu, Ngqika's father, who had never enjoyed power themselves. Ngqika gave them the task of taking care of one of his own sons. This enabled them to find an outlet for their ambitions by boosting their charge at the expense of his brothers, thereby assisting rather than obstructing the ruling chief. This institution was widely adopted by other chiefs since it resolved the structural conflict between the chief and his father's generation.

In 1800 Ngqika was at the height of his power. Ndlambe was his prisoner and although Hintsa had escaped, he did not pose any immediate threat to Ngqika's claim to be Paramount of Xhosaland. The minor chiefs either supported him or paid him tribute. He was fast extending his control over the councillors, and even dabbled in Thembu politics. One description of him runs as follows:

> *Gaika was a young man, at this time under twenty years of age, of an elegant form and a graceful and manly deportment; his height about five feet ten inches; his face of a deep bronze colour, approaching nearly to black; his skin, soft and smooth; his eyes dark brown and full of animation; his teeth regular, well-set and white as the purest ivory .... He seemed to be the adored object of his subjects; the name of Gaika was in every mouth, and it was seldom pronounced without symptoms of joy.*[2]

At about this time, Ngqika came under the influence of a Boer named Coenraad de Buys, known to the Xhosa as Khula ('the big one') because of his great height. Buys had fled from the British who had captured the Cape from the Dutch in 1795.

He made himself useful to Ngqika through his access to gun-powder, and demonstrated his freedom from race prejudice by making a mistress of Ngqika's mother and promising his daughter to the chief. He also contrived to prejudice Ngqika against the British, telling him that they were the 'bushmen of the sea'. This adverse impression was strengthened by the visit of the British emissary, Barrow, who thought to win Ngqika's friendship by a gift of tobacco, beads, pieces of copper and knives. Far from it: Ngqika was insulted, and said 'that they must consider the king of the Caffres in a very pitiful light if they could suppose his friendship was to be obtained by such trifles.'[3] He declared that there would be no peace with the British until the Boers imprisoned in Cape Town Castle were released. But Ngqika was no Boer puppet. He had defeated Ndlambe well before Buys's arrival, and he resisted the wilder anti-British schemes of the Boer refugees, such as invading the Colony to install Buys as king.

The War with Ndlambe

Ngqika's first major slip came in 1800, with the escape of Ndlambe from his custody. Ndlambe had been allowed to retain his wives and most of his cattle, but was forced to reside near Ngqika's Great Place under the eye of his nephew. He was treated with every respect and his advice was greatly valued, but Ndlambe remembered too well the days of his undisputed power. His position at the Great Place was weakened still further by the influence of Buys. Many of his supporters had fled into the Colony after Ngqika's victory, and they were joined by those who opposed Ngqika's centralizing measures. They sent messages to Ndlambe, urging him to join them. Matters came to a head when Ngqika asked Ndlambe to approve the murder of Ndlambe's brother, Siko, who he feared was con-spiring against him. Ndlambe refused, joined Siko and other rebels, and crossed the Fish river into the Colony. Here they became embroiled in the Third Frontier War (1799—1802) which was raging between the Colony and an alliance of rebel Khoi and minor Xhosa chiefs. Ndlambe had thus obtained his freedom from Ngqika at the expense of the antagonism of the Colony, whose territory he was occupying. Meanwhile, a quarrel had broken out between Ngqika's Khoi supporters and the Boers, with the result that Buys was forced to flee Xhosaland. Freed of Buys's influence and alive to the possibility of catching

Ndlambe between two fires, Ngqika made overtures to the British and returned stolen cattle and deserters to the Colony. Some of Ndlambe's supporters, including Siko, rejoined Ngqika and he recovered much of his former strength.

Ngqika now attempted to win the support of the colonial authorities. He promised that if the colonial authorities drove Ndlambe out of their territory and into his power, he would undertake to restore stolen cattle. Because he was not situated immediately on the border, Ngqika regarded the Colony not as a potential threat to himself but as a potential ally against Ndlambe, their common enemy. But by turning to an alien power to help subdue his own people, Ngqika set in train that certain logic of collaboration in which every step limits future options, creates further obligations, extracts further concessions and, in the end, becomes irreversible. At the time, however, Ngqika had no reason to believe that he was not master of the situation. Far from appearing overwhelmingly powerful, the Colonial authorities were so weak militarily that they were too afraid of Ndlambe to agree to Ngqika's plan. Ngqika was prepared to enter the Colony and attack his uncle himself, but the colonial landdrost (magistrate) dissuaded him. In order to provoke Ndlambe into leaving his colonial refuge, Ngqika took the unprecedented step of abducting one of his uncle's wives, the beautiful Thuthula (1807). In Xhosa terms, this was incest and it aroused a storm of indignation. Even Ngqika's steadfast supporters could not condone his action: 'You surely see that you are indeed mad,' they told him, 'nevertheless we shall lay down our lives for your madness.'

The war that followed was disastrous for Ngqika. According to one account he was left with only ten cows, and some of his children and those of his principal allies perished from hunger. Ngqika was only saved because several of the minor chiefs wished to keep the rivalry between himself and Ndlambe alive. They realized that the complete triumph of Ndlambe would lead to their own subjugation, and they therefore rejoined Ngqika. The war was terminated in 1808 with an agreement in which Ndlambe recognized Ngqika's seniority while the latter recognized his uncle's autonomy. But since Ndlambe continued to reside west of the Fish, he continued to provoke the resentment of the colonial authorities. In 1812, they finally expelled him from 'their' territory. Ngqika was no longer strong enough to take advantage of his enemy's weakness.

Ngqika Turns to the British for Aid

Ngqika's character deteriorated as his fortunes declined. In the period of his greatness, he had treated with the Dutch authorities as an equal and twice offered himself as an ally against the British. Gifts were exchanged on a formal basis, and Ngqika was perfectly ready to return them when he felt his honour demanded it. He 'drank wine with pleasure, but drank little.'[4] After the Thuthula débâcle, he became a mendicant both politically and materially, begging the colonial authorities for revenge on Ndlambe, and for clothes, cattle and brandy. In 1800 he was calling himself king of the Xhosa; in 1812, he received with anxious satisfaction the Colony's assurance that they regarded him as the greatest chief. He was not entirely without Xhosa allies, but his supporters were predators and political opportunists, men who were not satisfied to be loyal subordinates but not sufficiently powerful to compete with the leading chiefs. They were also the greatest plunderers, when it came to stealing colonial cattle. (A chief like Ndlambe was too aware of the political implications of cattle theft to permit it, except in cases of open hostility.) The interests of Ngqika's two allies—the Colony and the minor chiefs—were incompatible in the long run, but Ngqika managed to paper over the cracks by persuading the colonial authorities that Ndlambe was guilty of thefts committed by his own supporters.

Matters were brought to a head in 1817, when the Colonial Government decided to adopt a more aggressive policy to check the increase in cattle thefts which had resulted from the Xhosa expulsion of 1812. Governor Lord Charles Somerset offered Ngqika active military support against his Xhosa rivals in return for assistance in suppressing cattle-raiding. The proposal is remembered by Xhosa today as a succinct 'You protect me, and I'll protect you', but a contemporary Xhosa account of the conference in which the arrangement was finalized, gives a better picture of the conditions which dictated Ngqika's acceptance of the package:

> Ngqika said to the governor, 'There is my uncle and there are the other chiefs.' The governor then said, 'No, you must be responsible for all the cattle and the horses that are stolen.' The other chiefs then said to Ngqika, 'Say yes, that you will be responsible, for we see the man is getting angry.' for we had the cannon and artillerymen and soldiers and Boers with loaded muskets standing about us.[5]

Ngqika was by now so alienated from his own people that he could not rely on their support, and so far committed to the Colony that he could not turn back. In the end the combination of the carrot and the stick was too much for him, but he was at best an equivocal ally. He tried to make the most of his position by squeezing the maximum of presents out of the colonial authorities, while blaming Ndlambe for thefts which his own followers committed and which he often profited from himself.

Ndlambe was far from inactive. He followed a strongly nationalist line calculated to win followers from the compromised Ngqika. He won over the amaGqunukhwebe, the most important of the minor chiefdoms, and was reconciled with his estranged son, Mdushane. He was also able to call on the Paramountcy, which was beginning to reassert itself. Hintsa, who had slipped through Ngqika's fingers during his boyhood, was now grown up, and had succeeded in uniting the eastern Xhosa under his leadership. Bhurhu, Hintsa's brother, re-occupied the west bank of the Kei, and Hintsa began to consider extending his authority over the westernmost chiefdoms. He

2 Ngqika meeting Cape Governor Janssens

refused to recognize Ngqika and supported Ndlambe, whom he regarded as a loyal subordinate. To this impressive array of temporal and political power, Ndlambe was able to add the impressive magico-religious backing of Nxele ('Makanna'), who turned his influence against Ngqika, the incestuous adulterer, the friend of the whites, and the enemy of his patron, Ndlambe.

Ngqika countered as best he could be adopting a passive mystic named Ntsikana, who had already offered his services to Ndlambe. Ntsikana mocked at one of Nxele's more spectacular failures, an attempt to resurrect the dead, and warned the chiefs that they were endangering their privileges by honouring a commoner like Nxele. But he failed to inspire more than a small band of followers, who subsequently followed him into Christianity. An increasing number of Ngqika's followers joined Nxele, and Ngqika demanded that Ndlambe should hand him over. Ndlambe refused saying that Hintsa alone was king and that Ngqika was just a chief like himself and not entitled to give him orders. Ngqika answered that he too was a king, and sent a desperate message to his colonial allies for material support. It was too late. At the great battle of Amalinde (October 1818), Ngqika's forces were overwhelmed. Eventually, the colonial forces arrived, and the Fifth Frontier War (1818—19) commenced, culminating in Nxele's defeat at the gates of Grahamstown.

The Fruits of Collaboration

Ngqika's warriors assisted the colonial forces, and Ngqika and his eldest son, Maqoma, frequented the barracks, drinking, and dancing for the amusement of the troops. When the colonial forces reached the Kei river, Ngqika urged them to cross it and capture Hintsa, whom he claimed was deeply implicated in cattle-raiding. At long last, he appeared to be in sight of his objectives. But these were frustrated by a sudden switch of colonial policy. Not only did the colonial authorities refuse to cross the Kei, but Governor Somerset told Ngqika that he was appropriating Ngqika's own lands between the Kat and the Keiskamma rivers. This amazing decision—prompted partly by a racist inability to distinguish between friendly and hostile Xhosa, and partly by Somerset's desire to settle a party of Scots on the vacant land—sowed the seeds for the following Frontier War (1835—6). Ngqika protested that they were taking his birthplace, but he was ignored. As if this were not enough, the authorities demanded that Ngqika suppress the cattle-raiding which their latest land-confiscations had made inevitable. Ngqika agreed, but secretly encouraged raids and continued to share in the spoils, and attacked a mission station for informing on a party of horse-thieves. Somerset ordered Ngqika's arrest, but Ngqika escaped, dressed as a woman. For a short time, he verged on becoming the national leader of the Xhosa. Raiding was stepped up, and meetings were held with other chiefs to plan revenge.

But Ngqika was not the sort of man to save his honour at the expense of his political and material well-being. He lived in fear not only of his enemies but of the minor chiefs, who supported him for purely selfish reasons. He was even afraid of his capable son Maqoma, and leaned heavily on Tyhali, his son by a concubine, who sought to raise himself by acting as his father's hatchet-man. He hated his Great wife, Suthu, mother of his lame heir, Sandile. The colonial authorities had betrayed him, but they were the only friends he had. He came to accept his dependence and exploited it shamelessly, expanding his territory at the expense of the amaNdlambe and the minor chiefdoms. He used his reputation as a friend of the Colony to threaten other chiefs, including the Paramount himself, with commando attacks, and accused them of cattle-thieving in order to provoke the authorities. One incident, drawn from the last year of his life, illustrates the depths to which he had sunk. When his own son Maqoma incurred the displeasure of the colonial authorities by capturing some Thembu cattle, Ngqika 'strongly urged [the British Commandant] to go at once to Maqoma, without waiting to see whether he returns the Thembu cattle and attack him, fire upon him and his people and take his cattle, and then after that to reason with him.'[6]

Part of Ngqika's income was spent on attracting talented young warriors to his Great Place. Their military functions were underscored by the fact that they were known as *amasoldati* (soldiers) rather than as 'milkers of the Great Place', which was the name usually given to the chief's clients. This provided Ngqika with a permanent fighting-force, and he used it to raid his councillors and neighbouring chiefs for cattle. It was, of course, usual for a chief to exact tribute, and redistribute it among his subordinates. This was not merely a payment however, but a symbolic expression of his power and generosity, and it was used as a means of binding the people to their chief. This last innovation of Ngqika's—which did not survive him—created a mercenary corps for the purpose of extracting the wealth of his people for his personal benefit.

Whatever was not distributed to his followers, Ngqika spent on brandy. He might have echoed the reply of later Xhosa, who, on being reproached for heavy drinking, replied: We are already a crushed and destroyed people, and there is no use trying to preserve our nationality'.[7] Alcohol was a logical consequence of his moral capitulation. He purchased it, danced for it, 'sold' his wives for it, and ultimately died of it. He would do nothing unless he was paid for it, and even took to receiving his presents in private to avoid sharing them with his councillors.

Nxele died in 1820, attempting to escape from Robben Island, the prison of many subsequent generations of African nationalists. Ndlambe lingered on until February 1828, and died full of years and honour. When Ngqika died in 1829, reproached by his councillors and despised by his subjects, he retained only his great good looks—at the age of fifty, he still appeared thirty. Ravaged by liquor and, probably, tuberculosis, he was convinced that he had been bewitched and spent his final illness in the care of the diviners, often joining in as they danced for his recovery, and dancing till he collapsed. At the same time, the 'devoted' Tyhali spearheaded a hunt for witches, making full use of the opportunity to eliminate some of his own political opponents. It was indeed a macabre end for a reign that had commenced so auspiciously.

Conclusion

In their standard textbook, Oliver and Fage describe collaborators as 'far-sighted and well-informed men', while Ronald Robinson describes them as attracted by 'the allure of what the big society had to offer.'[8] Although it is possible to think of African leaders in South Africa who might fit this description— Moshoeshoe of the Sotho, Khama of the Tswana and Zibhebhu of the Zulu, for instance—Ngqika obviously belongs to another category. He did not feel inferior to Europeans on either the political or the social level. He certainly did not believe that a white skin entitled a man to special consideration. When a group of Boers reproached him for possessing a stolen horse, he broke off an important set of negotiations, explaining that he was not prepared to be 'messed on by dogs' such as the Boers. On a subsequent occasion, he disparaged a landdrost by saying 'He is a chief *made*, I am a chief *born*.'[9] European culture never appealed to him. He made rapid progress in reading and writing, but soon lost interest. He often asked visitors for articles, especially clothes, which caught his fancy, but never wore anything but traditional dress. His interest in Christianity was perfunctory, although he did his best to be polite to the missionaries and promised vaguely to send them a son for instruction. Paradoxical as it may seem, the man who perhaps did more than any other to undermine Xhosa resistance to white encroachment was passionately attached to his customs and traditions. This is well illustrated by his remarkable outburst to missionary Williams:

> *You have your manner to wash and decorate yourselves on the lord's day and I have mine, the same in which I was born and that I shall follow. I have given over a little to listen to your word but now I have done, for if I adopt your law I must surely overturn all my own and that I shall not do. I shall now begin to dance and praise my beast as much as I please, and I shall let all see who is the lord of this land.*[10]

Ngqika, together with Chief Samuel Maherero in Namibia, belongs to a category which, standing Oliver and Fage on their heads, collaborated because they were short-sighted and badly informed. He had no precedents to follow in his dealings with the Europeans, except those of Rharhabe and Ndlambe, both of whom had been willing to collaborate when the need arose. Ngqika failed to see that the fate of all the Xhosa was inextricably interwoven, and that collaboration with the enemy could only bring destruction to all. Because he did not fully comprehend the magnitude of the Europeans' challenge, he attempted to use them for his private purposes, with tragic consequences both for himself and for his nation.

NOTES

[1] N. C. Mhala, 'Ukuvela kwama-Ndlambe', in W. G. Bennie, ed., *Imibengo* (Lovedale, 1935).

[2] J. Barrow, *An Account of Travels into the Interior of Southern Africa* (2 vols., London, 1801–4), I, p. 151.

[3] H. Lichtenstein, *Travels in Southern Africa* (London, 1812, reprinted Cape Town, 2 vols., 1928–30), I, p. 402n.

[4] *Ibid.*, I, p. 395.

[5] *Report from the Select Committee on Aborigines (British Settlements)* (1836), I, p. 569: evidence of Tzatzoe.

[6] Cape Archives, C.O.366: H. Somerset to J. Bell, 6 March 1829.

[7] Cape of Good Hope, *Commission on Native Laws and Customs* (1883), 2 vols., I, p. 152.

[8] R. Oliver and J. D. Fage, *A Short History of Africa* (Harmondsworth, 1966), p. 203; R. Robinson, 'Non-European Foundations of European Imperialism: sketch for a theory of collaboration', in R. Owen and B. Sutcliffe, eds., *Studies in the Theory of Imperialism* (London, 1972), p. 120.

[9] L. Alberti, *Alberti's Account of the Xhosa in 1807* (English translation, Cape Town, 1968), p. 117; J. Campbell, *Travels in South Africa* (3rd edn., London, 1815), p. 371.

[10] B. Holt, *Joseph Williams and the Pioneer Mission to the South-Eastern Bantu* (Lovedale, 1954), p. 80.

FURTHER READING

J. H. Soga, *The South-Eastern Bantu* (Johannesburg, 1930).

H. Lichtenstein, *Travels in Southern Africa*, Vol. I (Cape Town, Van Riebeeck Society, 1928).

S. Kay, *Travels and Researches in Caffraria* (London, 1833)

D. Moodie, *The Record*, Part V (reprinted Cape Town, 1960).

J. T. Vanderkemp, 'Journals', *Transactions of the London Missionary Society*, Vol. I (London, 1800–04).

J. B. Peires, 'A History of the Xhosa, c. 1700–1835', M. A. thesis, Rhodes University, 1976.

2
Mzilikazi
c.1795–1868

Shaka carried a process of political centralization among
the peoples of the Natal-Zululand area to its conclusion,
creating with brutal force a large Zulu kingdom.
Mzilikazi, one of his generals, broke free from Shaka's
grip and fled north to found a new state, first in what is
now the Transvaal and then north of the Limpopo river,
in Zimbabwe.

Mzilikazi exploited both the creative opportunities and destruc-
tive possibilities presented by the Nguni diaspora to found the
Ndebele kingdom—one of the most formidable African states in
southern Africa in the nineteenth century. His state survived
and expanded through geographical mobility, parasitic means
and military might. Such negative means were not the only ones
Mzilikazi employed to guarantee the security and acceptance of
his state by the peoples encountered in his migration. Whenever
possible he used diplomacy both to achieve peace with his
external enemies and to subdue the locals in the various areas
where he settled. He also allowed the conquered people to
influence his state culturally, perhaps in order to foster a sense
of identity between the vanquished and his ruling elite. Mzilikazi's Ndebele state can be likened to a snowball that grew as it
rolled from present day Zululand through the Transvaal and
Botswana and finally settled in western Zimbabwe. It withstood
Boer and other ethnic incursions in the Transvaal and showed
resilience to fissiparous tendencies, such as the Thabayezinduna
and succession crises of 1840 and 1868.

Nothing is known definitely about the childhood of the
architect of this remarkable kingdom. Mzilikazi was born some
time between 1795 and 1800. He was of the Khumalo *sibongo*
(surname) and his chiefdom had risen during his father Matshobane's time as the result of segmentation from the rest of the

3 *Mzilikazi, from a drawing made by*
Cornwallis Harris in 1836

Khumalo clans. The chiefdom was located in the Ngotshe district of Natal, between the Kwebezi, a tributary of the Black Mfolozi, and Mkuzi rivers.

In the vicious struggle for supremacy, in what became Zulu-land, between Dingiswayo and later his successor Shaka on the one hand, and Zwide of the Ndwandwe on the other, the Khumalo of Matshobane first submitted to Zwide. Relationships between the Ndwandwe and the Khumalo were apparently strengthened by Mzilikazi's marriage to one of Zwide's daughters, who became his chief wife and bore him his heir Nkulumane. Zwide was apparently forced to murder Matshobane for betray-ing his overlord to the Zulu and to instal Mzilikazi as chief of the Khumalo.

After Shaka's destruction of the Ndwandwe power Mzilikazi transferred his allegiance to the up-and-coming Zulu nation. He was confirmed in his chieftainship, left occupying his territory and made commander of a regiment consisting mostly of his own people. In 1822 he led a raiding expedition against the Swazi but did not deliver the captured livestock to Shaka. When this act of disloyalty was discovered, Mzilikazi chose to flee the country rather that face a certain death penalty. By the end of 1823 he had crossed the Drakensberg mountains and was carv-ing out a new homeland on the Transvaal highveld. He settled in the country of the Pedi and the Kgatla, an area extending from the Ermelo district down the Olifants and perhaps Steelpoort rivers.

Small though his following of three hundred people was, Mzilikazi was able to subdue and incorporate many of the Kgatla and Pedi. He used the recently developed Zulu military organiza-tion, tactics and weapons, which were superior to anything known on the highveld. Furthermore, even though the Kgatla and the Pedi were numerically superior, they were politically fragmented into small chiefdoms, each of which was no larger than the invading Ndebele. These local factions may have had their own differences, so that some of them regarded Mzilikazi as an ally in settling scores against their neighbours. It also seems that the most important chiefdom in Pediland was weakened by a succession crisis following the death of its chief, Thulare, in 1823. In the struggle that ensued between Mzilikazi's people and the Thulare chiefdom, the latter were defeated. Some of the Thulare were forced to abandon their homeland, while the rest were probably incorporated into the Ndebele kingdom.

Finally, Mzilikazi increased his military dominance over the Kgatla and Pedi when he admitted into his following about one thousand Ndwandwe and other Nguni refugees from Zululand.

In 1825 Mzilikazi decided to shift the centre of his settlements westward. Drought played some part in forcing the westward migration of the Ndebele, but it seems Mzilikazi's fear of other Nguni raiding states was the main reason. First, Zwide had settled in the Olifants-Steelpoort area and, though no evidence is available to show that the Ndebele and Zwide's fugitives ever clashed, it is not unlikely that Zwide would have liked to punish Mzilikazi for co-operating with Shaka. Secondly, there was Nxaba, also a fugitive Ndwandwe, who actually attacked Mzilikazi in 1825, and thirdly, Sobhuza I was busy building the future Swazi nation. Even though Sobhuza avoided raiding powerful states, he frequently attacked the weak Pedi chiefdoms, so that both the nascent Ndebele and Swazi states may have found themselves sharing raiding grounds.

Whatever factors may have influenced Mzilikazi, he nonetheless established in 1825 his capital called Mhlahlandlela in the Magaliesberg hills near the Crocodile river. Perhaps this area stretching from present-day Pretoria to Rustenburg was chosen for dense settlement; villages and towns were more thinly scattered down the Crocodile to its junction with the Marico river. The local people consisted of the Kgatla and Hurutshe and Southern Ndebele and by using diplomatic persuasion and force, Mzilikazi conquered and incorporated some of these original inhabitants. Die-hard Kgatla and other Tswana were forced to flee westward. Mzilikazi was so successful in increasing his following by absorbing the local inhabitants that by 1829 his army was estimated at 1,400 soldiers. With his fast growing army he raided the Sotho and Tswana living between the Vaal and the Limpopo for livestock, and sent raiding expeditions to the Shona country across the Limpopo and that of the Sotho to the south of the Vaal river.

Mzilikazi's problems of insecurity were not removed by his westward migration. If anything they seemed to grow worse. He was attacked by the Griqua leaders Jan Bloem and Berend Berends and by the Zulu, Dingane. In 1828, when most of his forces were away from the country on a raiding expedition, Jan Bloem invaded the country with a force consisting of Korana, Bergenaar, Taung and Rolong. The attackers rounded up a large amount of livestock, but were caught up by the Ndebele army as they made off. The Ndebele recovered some of the cattle although the raiders escaped. Berend Berends was the next to organize a military expedition, made up of Korana and Griqua, with a view to destroying the Ndebele kingdom, but he fared no better than his Griqua predecessor. He captured a number of cattle but the Ndebele army retook them. These southern invasions forced Mzilikazi to place a guarding force along the Vaal river and made him suspicious of anyone approaching his country from that direction.

Even more formidable a force was the new Zulu king, Dingane, who had in 1828 murdered Shaka and taken over power. He apparently was as keen as his predecessor to punish Mzilikazi for breaking away from the Zulu nation. Probably the nearby raiding grounds had been denuded of booty, so that the Transvaal highveld teeming with Ndebele livestock presented the only promising alternative. A war against Mzilikazi might also divert attention from the domestic political situation, for many were dissatisfied with Dingane's means of getting himself into power. Thus in 1832 Dingane's army invaded Ndebeleland and destroyed three military centres. The Pedi, who had not been fully assimilated into the Ndebele nation, took advantage of the ensuing confusion to regain their independence by returning to their homeland in the Olifants-Steelpoort area. Mzilikazi was again forced to move west in order to increase the distance between himself and the formidable Zulu.

Geographical mobility and military might, as already pointed out, were not the only means Mzilikazi tried to achieve security on the highveld. He also sought to gain the friendship of the white missionaries and traders, who might not only supply him with firearms but also become a counterweight to the Griqua. Two Scots traders, Robert Schoon and William McLuckie, visited him soon after Bloem's attack of 1828 and familiarized him with firearms. The traders were willing to put in a good word for Mzilikazi with the London Missionary Society and Wesleyan missionaries working at Kuruman and at Plaatberg. Mzilikazi himself displayed anxiety to establish firm contacts with friendly whites by sending his own ambassador Mncumbata Khumalo to Kuruman, possibly with an invitation to Robert Moffat to visit Ndebeleland. In 1829 Moffat visited Mzilikazi and the two men became fast friends for many years to come. Mzilikazi was not interested in Moffat's religious teachings. He wanted the latter's assistance and advice in his dealings with the Europeans

4 *First reception by Mzilikazi, 1835*

and, if possible, to use Moffat as a source of firearms. Indeed after 1832, when he was settled in the Marico district, he continued to treat visiting traders and hunters well. He even permitted American missionaries to settle at Mosega in order to teach his people Christianity.

Unfortunately for Mzilikazi, his shift westward and his friendship with European traders and missionaries did not save him from the Boer invaders. These were white settlers, who were also in search of new homelands. They approached his country in large numbers and unannounced. Mzilikazi's immediate reaction was to regard them as an enemy to be resisted at all costs. In August 1836 Mzilikazi's patrolling troops managed to wipe out Boer families and servants they caught unawares and to take away their wagons. But the next Boer party to be attacked had a chance to form a laager, from which effective shield they were able to kill one hundred Ndebele soldiers and repulse the assailants. Such a reverse by a Boer party of thirty-five men must have proved to Mzilikazi that he was up against a formidable enemy indeed. His national army at this time consisted of just over five thousand men. Perhaps in an effort to destroy the Boer menace once and for all, Mzilikazi decided on 18 October 1836 to pitch almost all his forces against the invaders. On 19 October the four thousand strong army attacked a Boer laager at Vegkop in the Northern Free State. The Ndebele failed dismally to penetrate the wagon fortress and lost 430 soldiers. They did however capture all the Boer livestock, consisting of one hundred horses, 4,600 head of cattle, and over 50,000 sheep and goats. Mzilikazi's military action only succeeded in temporarily warding off the white settlers, for on 17 January 1837 a Boer commando invaded his country, killed four hundred soldiers and an unspecified number of women and children, and made off with six thousand head of cattle.

This was followed in June by a Zulu invasion, during which Mzilikazi lost an even larger number of soldiers and cattle. This last attack forced him to abandon the country south of the Limpopo. As he organized his people for migration in November 1837, the Boers again caught up with him and in nine days slew something like three thousand Ndebele. It is a fair guess that in the twelve months that Mzilikazi tried to defend his homeland south of the Limpopo he lost almost half of his army. Moreover, many Sotho-Tswana remained when Mzilikazi moved to western Zimbabwe, so that only 15,000 people followed him.

When Mzilikazi decided to leave the Limpopo-Vaal area he was in his late thirties or early forties. He was of medium height, slightly fat, but with a decidedly tough and athletic build. His effeminate voice, apparent absent-mindedness and affability belied a shrewd, calculating and sometimes ruthless mind. He was brave and indeed a military hero and was revered as such by his people. In his old age when the *imbongi* (praiser) recounted the battles His Majesty had fought and the formidable and lesser chiefs he had either repulsed or subdued, and finally underlined the king's military prowess, Mzilikazi was wont to shed tears over the fact that he was now unable to lead his army personally.

Mzilikazi did not use his *ubuqawe* (bravery) for savage destruction, but used his power to defend whatever he had and to build. War was indeed an instrument of construction and defence. This was shown by the rapid expansion of his state. In the Limpopo-Vaal area his people were estimated to be between 60,000 and 80,000, an incredible rate of growth considering that fourteen years previously his following had been three hundred. This state was wealthy too, teeming with herds of cattle and flocks of sheep and goats. Both livestock and people were gathered from as far afield as Shonaland and present day Lesotho in order to construct a powerful Ndebele state. Thus by the time Mzilikazi made his home in western Zimbabwe he was an experienced statebuilder.

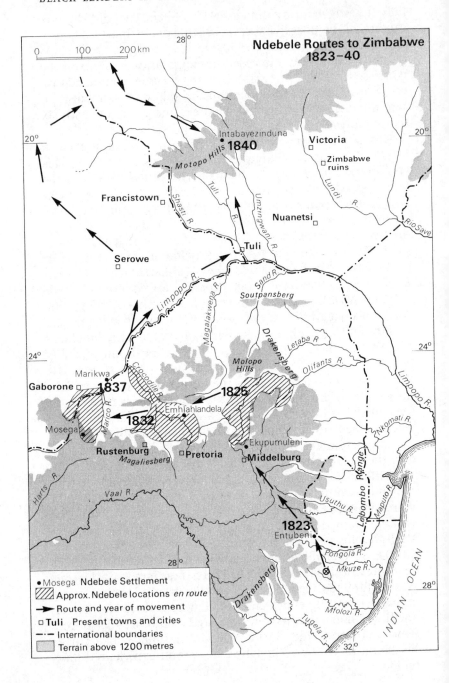

Ndebele Routes to Zimbabwe
1823–40

Zimbabwe

The migration to Zimbabwe was a terrible experience for Mzilikazi. The nation threatened to break up. At the Chwapong Hills in modern Botswana, Mzilikazi split his nation into two groups which were to follow different routes in order to find sufficient water. One group led by Gundwane Ndiweni travelled with the heir Nkulumane, and Mzilikazi himself led the second group. For almost two years the two groups had no contact with each other. Gundwane settled around *Thabayezinduna*, the flat-topped hill eleven miles from modern Bulawayo. Meanwhile Mzilikazi travelled through Lake Ngami and probably tried to approach the Zambesi, but was driven back by the tsetse fly, which killed his herds by the hundred. He then entered his new country through the Makarikari Lake. By the time the two groups rejoined each other in 1840, Gundwane and other chiefs had started to instal Nkulumane as their king. The excuse given was that they had already started growing crops and needed a king who could lead them in the ceremony of the first fruits, which was also conducted to purify the nation.

Mzilikazi regarded the installation of his son in his lifetime as an act of rebellion by the chiefs concerned. Indeed it was more than a revolt: it reflected the uneasy unity of the Ndebele state. Mzilikazi had managed to weld together the people he conquered on the Transvaal highveld and in Shonaland by destroying them as political entities and then absorbing them into his state as individuals. As much as possible, incorporated people were distributed into different regiments and localities, thereby preventing the growth of powerful sub-ethnic loyalties. However, he did not do this with the Nguni refugees that joined him on the highveld.

He admitted eight chiefdoms which continued to be ruled by their own leaders. A classic case was that of the Zwangendaba people, ruled by the Masuku clan of Mbiko kaMadlenya. This group joined the Ndebele state in the Transvaal and Mzilikazi built a powerful regiment out of it. We do not know what part this group played in the 1840 crisis but we know that in 1868, after Mzilikazi's death, it led the opposition faction to Lobengula and even questioned the right of the Khumalo clan to produce kings for the Ndebele nation. It is more than likely therefore that when the eight chiefs *Konza'd* to Mzilikazi they did so without abandoning their hope of one day setting up their own separate states.

Of course, the Ndebele nation had become complex through the absorption of diverse ethnic groups whose loyalty lay primarily with Mzilikazi. Gundwane and his fellow conspirators could not hive off by making one of themselves king of their faction. To carry almost everyone along they needed some vestiges of Mzilikazi's leadership, and these they found in the young Nkulumane and his mother. Even with such precautions the secessionist leaders failed to gain the support of all the chiefs. Gwabalanda Mate, one of Mzilikazi's trusted councillors and chief of the Amhlope division and province, dissociated himself completely from the whole scheme, choosing instead to look after Lobengula, the second possible successor to Mzilikazi. Mzilikazi dealt with the crisis with characteristic ruthlessness. The secessionist leaders were tried and either executed or forced to flee. The fate of Nkulumane is unknown. Some say he was either killed with the rest of the rebels or was executed years later on the orders of Mzilikazi and others say he was sent to go and live with his maternal relatives of Zwide in the south. However, the fact that later searches in South Africa failed to produce the heir, except the pretender Kanda, makes it seem likely that Nkulumane was killed on his father's orders. Indeed, the fact that Lobengula, who later succeeded Mzilikazi, only survived the executions by being hidden by Gwabalanda Mate, first in his town Mhlahlandlela and later among the *Mwari* priests, makes it certain that His Majesty was intent upon wiping out, and did in fact kill, most of his children who were likely to succeed him. This was to remove the danger of fissiparous factions emerging around his possible successors during his lifetime.

At the same time as he was dealing with this internal political crisis, Mzilikazi had to contend with the Shona, the original inhabitants of Zimbabwe. In carving out his new homeland the Ndebele king had to pursue both a violent and a pacific policy. By the time he had reorganized his state in Zimbabwe his wealth had been depleted seriously. Some of his cattle had been taken from him by the Zulu and the Boers on the highveld, a lot must have been eaten by the Ndebele themselves as they had no time to raise crops during the migration, and many more had been weeded out by the lethal tsetse fly in the Zambesi valley. This made it necessary for Mzilikazi to try and rebuild his wealth by raiding the Shona. The Nyubi living in the Matopo area were raided for grain. Mzilikazi exercized further violence on the Shona polities in order to destroy them as political units, so as to produce individuals for incorporation into his state. As we saw, only 15,000 people migrated with him, and probably many of these died during the march. Thus, it was necessary to employ force against the Shona in order to obtain recruits for his army and women to produce children.

However it must be stressed that Mzilikazi did not pursue a consistently violent policy towards the Shona. There were factors militating against antagonizing the local population too much. His own political weakness, so forcefully demonstrated by the Thabayezinduna crisis, influenced him against an aggressive foreign policy. Moreover, he had to contend for his new home with an equally militaristic and powerful group, the Swazi of Queen Nyamazana. The formidable Nyamazana, who some oral evidence says was responsible for the destruction of the Rozvi empire, apparently originally migrated with Nxaba and remained in Zimbabwe when the rest of the group went to the north of the Zambesi. Mzilikazi eventually overcame the Swazi factor by his marriage to Nyamazana, which united the Ndebele and the Swazi.

In addition, the Boers were still a real threat, and in fact, as if to demonstrate that Mzilikazi was not out of their reach, they invaded his country in 1847. Mzilikazi also had an almost paranoiac fear of the Zulu. It is clear that he never believed that he was out of the reach of the Zulu army. In 1866, for instance, he assembled the whole nation and wanted to abandon western Zimbabwe because the Zulu were rumoured to be about to attack his kingdom. It was only after his councillors had reassured him of their capacity to resist the invaders and when the priest had propitiated both the national ancestral spirits and *Molimo* (God) that he abandoned the idea of migration. All these problems of insecurity forced Mzilikazi to use violence sparingly against the Shona.

Mzilikazi's policy of mixed violence and diplomatic persuasion met with spectacular success because of the Shona political situation. His Nguni predecessors, the Ngoni of Zwangendaba, the Nxaba and the Swazi of Nyamazana had done much to undermine Shona political unity. Nyamazana's forces, for instance, had defeated the Rozvi army at the capital Manyanga, and had wounded the ruler Chirisamhuru so severely that he eventually died. The death of Chirisamhuru and the rest of the misfortunes of the political centre resulted in the independence of the chiefdoms that had constituted the basic political units of the Rozvi empire. One Tohochipi succeeded to this tottering Rozvi dynasty but failed dismally to unite the Shona against the Ndebele intruders.

Each Shona chief decided to organize his own resources to meet Ndebele onslaughts. This left Mzilikazi in a good position to pick off the Shona chiefs one by one and force them either into submission or abandoning their homeland. Tohochipi himself was compelled to retreat to the Mavange hills in the east, before being defeated and captured in 1866. Other Rozvi aristocratic local rulers such as Mtinhima of the Malugwana mountains and Dlembewu of the northern part of the Doro range were attacked and defeated. Some of their followers became Ndebele subjects while others fled further eastward. Several Shona chiefdoms saw the futility of resistance and responded to Mzilikazi's persuasions by submitting to his rule. Such chiefdoms were rewarded with important positions in the kingdom, such as the collection of tributes from other Shona people. By this process Mzilikazi was able to dominate politically the whole area between the Gwanda district in the south and Zambezi in the north, the Makarikari depression in west and the Umniati and Mtirikwe rivers in the east.

Mzilikazi's military power and ability to shift his people in order to elude his enemies were largely the result of the way he organized his state. Whether in South Africa or in western Zimbabwe he always adopted the agglomerated pattern of settlement. In the new homeland the settlements were first concentrated within a few miles of Thabayezinduna. Even when the population expanded, villages never split far from the small area of the headwaters of the Mguza, Bembesi, Mzingwane and the Gwai rivers. The limited extent of the country reflected its highly centralized structure. Mzilikazi controlled almost every important aspect of his people's lives, to the extent of making his nation a family and himself the head of it. His word was law, particularly in the early years. European observers often remarked that every event, from the death of a cow to the death of a chief, was reported to Mzilikazi, who in turn kept abreast of the conditions of his people by paying regular visits to all the important towns and villages. In addition he had as his most efficient channel of news the hierarchical structure of appointed officials as well as his two hundred wives, who were distributed in all the chief towns.

Mzilikazi was able to achieve this striking degree of centralization by identifying his military organization with the whole civil administrative machinery so that the two were indistinguishable. This manifested itself in the fact that the army and the population could not be distinguished. Though no definite boundaries existed in the new homeland, the country had roughly four provinces, coinciding with the four army divisions: the Amhlope in the centre, the Amakanda in the east, the Amnyama in the south, and the Igapa in the west. Each province further consisted of *amabuto* (regiments). At the head of each province or division was an *induna enkulu*, while each *ibuto* was administered by an *induna*. Apart from original Nguni chiefs, most of these military-cum-administrative officials were appointed by Mzilikazi himself. He personally trained or supervised the formation of a new *ibuto* and at the completion of the training he gave the *ibuto* its name, cattle for milking, a piece of land for settlement, women to cook for it, and appointed a commander who was also its chief. The commander therefore held his position at Mzilikazi's pleasure, while his *ibuto* and himself were dependent upon his majesty for their supply of milk and meat, as the king allowed them to eat the beef of beasts that died on their own.

Despite the centralized nature of the state, Mzilikazi's was not a one-man government. He was assisted by two councils: the *Mphakathi*, made up of some members of the royal family and elders chosen for their great knowledge of traditional customs, and the *Izikulu*, a larger assembly of all the *izinduna zamabuto*.

Mzilikazi also tried to weld his followers together, allowing different cultural influences. In South Africa he was beginning to adopt *Molimo*, the Tswana god, when the process was interrupted by his migration. In western Zimbabwe he freely employed Shona doctors to treat him for his ailments and further adopted the *Mwari*-cult for rainmaking purposes. He was of course careful to preserve his original religious practices. He continued to hold the annual *Inxwala* ceremony during which the nation was renewed and during which he prayed to his ancestral spirits for protection and victory against his enemies.

In 1859 Mzilikazi took the bold step of allowing missionaries to settle in his new country. He gave them a piece of land to build a mission station at Inyati, one of his chief towns, but until the death of Mzilikazi in 1868 the missionaries achieved nothing in terms of converting the people. The white teachers blamed

Mzilikazi for their failure, but there is no evidence to show that he actually prohibited his people from accepting Christianity. The fact was that the local religious system satisfied the spiritual needs of the people. The cultural changes that were being demanded by the mission, such as abandoning polygamy in favour of monogamy, were unacceptable to the Ndebele. However, by letting missionaries into the country Mzilikazi saddled his nation with an element that in the late nineteenth century would become allied with the forces that destroyed his kingdom.

In 1868 Mzilikazi died. His people mourned him, saying, *'Intaba seyidilikile'* ('The Mountain has fallen'). He had been indeed a tower of courage. His lasting achievement was the building of a kingdom that survived all internal and external pressures until destroyed by European settlers in 1893. He also changed the ethnic composition of modern Zimbabwe, which prior to his coming had been predominantly Shona. If today the political leaders of Zimbabwe are assiduously trying to overcome problems of ethnicity and to achieve unity among their people, they are dealing with some of the lasting legacies of Mzilikazi.

FURTHER READING

R. Kent Rasmussen, *Mzilikazi of the Ndebele* (London, 1977).

A. T. Bryant, *Olden Times in Zululand and Natal* (London, 1929).

W. F. Lye, 'The Ndebele Kingdom South of the Limpopo river', *Journal of African History*, X, I, 1969.

'Mziki' (A. A. Campbell), *Mlimo: the Rise and Fall of the Matabele* (Pietermaritzburg, 1926).

R. Kent Rasmussen, *Migrant Kingdom: Mzilikazi's Ndebele in South Africa* (London, 1978)

3
Mpande kaSenzangakhona
c. 1798—1872

Shaka's successor Dingane fought the Voortrekkers who entered Natal in 1837. After his defeat at their hands, his half-brother joined forces with the Trekkers against him. In return Mpande was recognized as ruler north of the Thukela river. There Mpande successfully maintained the Zulu kingdom in the face of both internal and external challenges, ruling it for over three decades, more than half its total life-span.

Mpande ruled the Zulu kingdom from 1840 until his death in 1872. For nearly thirty-three years he maintained his position as head of one of the most powerful states in southern Africa and helped steer it through a time of unprecedentedly rapid and far-reaching political change. Throughout his reign he had to struggle to keep together a nation beset by internal conflicts, and by pressures emanating from the Boer and British communities that had been established in the 1840s on its western and southern boundaries. Neither Shaka nor Dingane before him had faced problems of similar complexity, and there was nothing in Mpande's early life to indicate that he possessed the qualities needed to deal with them. In the event he proved an able enough leader to preserve the integrity of his kingdom through a period longer than the reigns of the three other Zulu kings combined. His talents have been given scant recognition in the history books, which usually depict him as an indolent simpleton who exercised little real power. Certainly he was no great warrior figure like his brother Shaka, but his ability to grasp the changing realities of his position as head of the Zulu nation qualified him to lead it through times which demanded the skills of the politician and diplomat rather than of the fighter.

5 Mpande, from a painting
by George French Angas, c.1848

Very little is known of Mpande's life before he became king. He was born in about 1798, the son of Senzangakhona kaJama, hereditary ruler of the small Zulu chiefdom, and his ninth wife, Songiya kaNgotsha of the Hlabisa people. On the death of Senzangakhona in about 1816, the Zulu chiefship was usurped by Shaka, and the young prince Mpande was incorporated into the reorganized Zulu army. Nothing is known of his role in the momentous events of the next few years when Shaka and his army were carving out the new Zulu kingdom, though by his own account he held a position of command and served in a number of campaigns. As the power of the Zulu royal house expanded, so was the position of Mpande enhanced. His royal birth made him one of the more important figures in the kingdom, and therefore one closely watched by the king for signs of wavering loyalty. By maintaining a submissive posture he was able to satisfy the royal scrutiny, and shortly before Shaka's assassination in 1828 he was allowed to marry at what was in the Zulu kingdom a relatively early age, being presented with his first wife by the king himself.

If the position of a prince of the royal house had been precarious under Shaka, it was much more so under his successor Dingane, who had even less reason to trust the loyalty of his close male relatives. At the time of Shaka's death Mpande was away on the ill-fated campaign against Soshangane, and on his return he seems to have given his allegiance to Dingane without hesitation. But why the morbidly suspicious new king allowed him to survive as a potential rival when several of his brothers were summarily disposed of is not clear. The usual view is that he was spared because of his docility and apparent harmlessness, but by itself this is not a sufficient explanation. Another suggestion is that a certain stigma which attached to Mpande's birth lulled Dingane into believing that neither he nor his sons would ever be acceptable to the Zulu people as king. Yet another argument is that Dingane in fact allowed Mpande to live in order to produce the heir to the throne whom he himself dared not father. Whatever the reason, Mpande was allowed to live quietly at his homestead or *umuzi* near Eshowe in the south of the Zulu country, to take a number of wives, and to build up something of a personal following. He appears to have played little, if any, part in public affairs, but his position near the trading route to Port Natal, and near the increasingly sensitive southern border, was one of some importance.

6 *Dingane and his dog, Makwilana*

The arrival of the Voortrekkers in Natal in 1837 inaugurated a new era in the history of the Zulu kingdom and in the fortunes of Mpande. Up till this time Dingane had had no reason to suspect his loyalty, but after the outbreak of war with the Trekkers and the crushing defeat of the Zulu forces at the Ncome (Blood) river in 1838, Mpande began to emerge as an alternative focus of allegiance. A number of leading men in the kingdom were dissatisfied with their position under Dingane and hoped, by ousting him, to assert their power over a new king. There is no evidence as to what action Mpande took to build up support for himself, but at this time of political crisis his mere existence as a potential rival might well have been enough to doom him in Dingane's eyes. In about August 1839 the king found an excuse for summoning Mpande to appear before him. Mpande must have been preparing for this eventuality for some time, and a secret warning, apparently stemming from one of Dingane's most senior councillors, that the king intended to kill him, was enough to spur him into action. In September 1839, with a following estimated by some as consisting of nearly half the Zulu nation, he fled south across the Thukela to seek the protection of the fledgling republic of Natalia.

This event, one of the most decisive in the history of the kingdom, is still remembered among the Zulu as 'the breaking of the rope that held the nation together'. But it did more than split the kingdom into two factions: it gave the Trekkers in Natal the chance to intervene decisively in Zulu affairs and so introduce a new element into the nation's political life. By his own account to the Volksraad in Pietermaritzburg it seems that Mpande was not necessarily hoping for a military alliance against Dingane, and would have been content to remain in Natal and submit to Trekker authority in return for land and protection. But the flight to Natal of no less a person than the brother of the Zulu king, together with a large force of fighting men, gave the Trekkers an unexpected opportunity to reopen the struggle with Dingane. Their immediate motives were to avenge the deaths of their compatriots killed by the Zulu the year before, and to extract compensation for their losses of cattle, but they hoped also to instal Mpande as a puppet king in Dingane's place. At the end of October 1839 an official Trekker delegation proceeded to Mpande's temporary settlement near the Thongathi river, formally recognized him as head of the Zulu refugees, and made an alliance with him against Dingane.

Military action against Dingane followed a few months later. In January 1840 Mpande's army, led by Nongalaza kaNondela, defeated Dingane's forces in a fierce battle at Maqongqo in the north of the Zulu country. Some days later the victorious army was joined by a commando from Natal. After a fruitless pursuit of Dingane, the Trekkers returned to the allied camp on the Black Mfolozi and there, on 10 February, Commandant-General Andries Pretorius proclaimed Mpande king of the Zulu. In turn Mpande swore loyalty to the Volksraad. Four days later Pretorius proclaimed the annexation to the republic of all the Zulu territory between the Thukela and the Black Mfolozi, and then, driving its booty of more than 30,000 cattle, the commando returned to Natal. Five months after fleeing for his life from Dingane, Mpande had become king of the Zulu nation.

Consolidation of the New Regime

So long as Dingane remained alive Mpande could never be certain of retaining the kingship that he had usurped, but a few months after Maqongqo the fugitive former king was murdered by the Nyawo people near the Lubombo mountains, and Mpande could feel more secure. His most pressing need was to consolidate his authority over a nation in which civil war had loosened or broken pre-existing ties of allegiance to the king, and had greatly weakened his position in relation to his leading subject chiefs and *izinduna*. Mpande had been carried to power by an alliance of subordinate chiefs, and could rule effectively only with their support. These men kept him in office and at the same time vied with him and with one another for power, while for his part Mpande was constantly trying to enhance his position by playing off his subordinates against one another. The story of Zulu domestic affairs during his reign is very much the story of the king's political struggles with his chiefs and *izinduna*. As described below, in the 1850s these struggles became interlocked with a succession dispute between two of the king's sons, but at issue throughout was the question of who was to exercise authority in the land.

An important effect of this rivalry was to decentralize political power in the kingdom, thereby tempering the despotism of the Zulu monarchy. Though Mpande wielded autocratic power, and arbitrary killings continued in his reign, his system of government was considerably more relaxed than that of his two predecessors. But this was not due solely to internal factors. Unlike Shaka and Dingane, Mpande had powerful white-dominated communities as neighbours, whose presence helped check the tendency of the Zulu kingdom to break up into its constituent parts. Where Shaka and Dingane had frequently resorted to methods of terror to hold the kingdom together, Mpande could afford to rule with a lighter land, in the knowledge that his subjects could not now easily desert him. Though a flow of refugees from the Zulu kingdom into Natal in the early years of his reign caused him some concern, it was never large enough to threaten to undermine his power.

If, paradoxically, the presence of the Boers and British on the Zulu borders helped to maintain Mpande's authority, it eventually came to pose a serious threat to the existence of his kingdom. The Boers saw the fertile and productive Zulu country as a means of satisfying their land hunger, and of providing the access to the sea that would help render them independent of British domination. Certain British interests for their part came to want control over the Zulu country in order the more effectively to maintain British supremacy in southern Africa. In Mpande's time neither Boers nor British had the manpower or resources to subdue and colonize the powerful state which he had inherited from Shaka and Dingane, but both sought to extend their influence over the kingdom by gaining a hold on its ruler. Mpande welcomed them as the allies he needed to help secure his position against internal challenges, but at the same time sought to exploit their conflicting objectives to preserve his own independence.

The demise of the republic of Natalia in 1842 removed the shadowy suzerainty which the Trekkers had claimed to exercise over the Zulu kingdom, and encouraged Mpande to get rid of his closest rival for the kingship. By 1843 a dissident party with the powerful backing of Mawa, Senzangakhona's sister, seems to have been forming round the person of the king's only surviving brother, Gqugqu, who though younger than Mpande, apparently had a stronger genealogical claim to the throne. In May or June 1843 a force sent by Mpande wiped out him and his family, upon which Mawa and several thousand followers fled over the Thukela into Natal. The flight of these and other refugees was potentially an inflammatory issue in Mpande's dealings with the newly formed colony of Natal, but when the British commissioner Henry Cloete visited him in October 1843 it was agreed that refugees from the Zulu country should be allowed to remain in Natal, and that any cattle which they took with them should be returned to the king. Another important point of agreement was that the boundary between the Zulu country and Natal would henceforth be the line of the Thukela and Mzinyathi (Buffalo) rivers. The claim of the republic of Natalia to the land extending from the Thukela to the Black Mfolozi was tacitly dropped, although Cloete secured the nominal cession of St Lucia bay to the British crown.

The new border did not immediately become stabilized. It is unlikely, given his first-hand observations of white military capabilities, that Mpande ever seriously contemplated an attack on the colony, but he was no doubt concerned to feel out the strength of the British, who were still largely an unknown quantity to African societies outside the eastern Cape frontier zone. At the same time he kept his options open by seeking to remain on good terms with the Boers. By 1847 he was secretly negotiating with a group of them who were trying to set up a separate republic in northern Natal. When the Natal government acted to assert its authority in the area, Mpande hastily backed away from further involvement, but as late as 1848, when a Zulu force crossed into Natal, trying to head off the fugitive Hlubi chief Langalibalele, he does not seem to have been too concerned about offending the weak colonial administration. Like every other African leader in the sub-continent, Mpande had been watching for the outcome of the Boer-British conflict that had broken into the open in 1842. However, it was not until a British force had defeated a rebellious Boer faction at Boomplaats in the Orange River Sovereignty in August 1848, that Mpande would have become aware of the extent of British power in southern Africa, and adjusted his foreign policies accordingly. Though he never abandoned his policy of maintaining good relations with the Boers, he was henceforth careful not to provoke the British. From this time onward, in spite of occasional scares on both sides, the Thukela-Mzinyathi line remained one of the most stable black-white frontiers in southern African until it was violated by the British in 1879.

7 *A Zulu hunting dance, from a painting by George French Angas, c.1848*

The Challenge from Within

The late 1840s and early 1850s were the years of Mpande's greatest strength. At home, he had eliminated his closest rivals, and his sons were not yet old enough to challenge him. Abroad, he had established a working relationship with the British in Natal, and the Boers on his north-western borders were as yet too involved in their own domestic disputes to pose a threat to the Zulu country. An indication of the king's self-assurance at this time may perhaps be seen in his decision in 1850 to allow missionaries, whom he had forced to suspend operations in 1842, to resume work in his country, but it would in any case have been difficult to keep them out when white fortune-seekers were beginning to cross the Thukela in some numbers. The Zulu kingdom's wealth in cattle and game had attracted traders and hunters since the 1820s, and the large-scale immigration of British settlers into Natal in the years 1849—51 gave a considerable impetus to commerce between the Zulu country and Port Natal. Though there were times, as during the political crisis of 1856—61, when the entry of traders and hunters into the Zulu country was discouraged or even prohibited, in general the regulations governing their activities seem to have been much more relaxed than in Dingane's day. The effects of their commercial operations still need to be studied in detail; in general it seems fair to say that they did not have any fundamental impact on the structure of Zulu society. Research is also needed on the extent to which the new patterns of trade affected the old ones on which they were super-imposed. While the trade from Port Natal was of growing importance in the mid-19th century, the Zulu still kept up their centuries-old traffic with the Portuguese at Delagoa Bay, trading through Tsonga middlemen for copper, brass, firearms, and spirits in exchange for cattle, sheep, and goats.

Zulu society in Mpande's time was by no means unchanging, as it has often been portrayed, but in essence it remained based on the institutions evolved in Shaka's reign. The army continued to play a pivotal role in the lives of the whole population, though after the establishment of Boer and British communities on the kingdom's borders it had few opportunities for campaigning. Age-grades of young men and women continued to be enrolled every few years, with a dozen or more male and five or six female 'regiments' being formed in the course of Mpande's reign. Marriage remained contingent on the king's permission. Regiments were required to live in specially erected military barracks or *amakhanda*, each under the control of a female member of the Zulu royal house. Given the more peaceful conditions of existence of the time, it seems that young men were not required to serve continuously as in Shaka's and Dingane's time: to this extent one can perhaps talk of Zulu society in Mpande's reign as becoming partly demilitarized.

The king ruled with the advice, and under the influence, of his sub-chiefs and *izinduna*. Most powerful of these by the 1850s was Masiphula kaMamba of the emGazini clan, a close relative of the Zulu royal house, and a formidable personality. Described by Bishop Colenso in 1859 as 'a sly, deep, cunning fellow', Masiphula commanded considerable respect in the nation, and retained his position of pre-eminence till the end of the king's long reign.

Mpande lived at his capital of Nodwengu in the Mahlabathini area north of the White Mfolozi. During his reign this *umuzi* was rebuilt a number of times at different sites. In 1859 Colenso recorded it as having a cattle enclosure with a diameter of over

700 yards, 1,000 houses, and a population of 2,500, which would have made it one of the largest towns in south-eastern Africa. Here the king held his court and councils, reviewed his troops, inspected his herds of cattle, and performed major public ceremonies. In later life obesity and illness required him to be drawn in a little cart by his subjects when he wanted to move any distance. His fondness of the pleasures of court life were reflected in a line from one of the songs sung by his people, 'Abandon your beer pots, O King!', but as long as he was physically able, he participated in the dancing and singing at public festivals, and was known as a good reciter of praises. Though vain and fond of personal ornamentation, his self-control in public was strong, and even when angry or excited he spoke with restraint. In his time, as befitted a king, he married some twenty wives, and fathered over fifty children.

The early 1850s saw the beginning of a decline in Mpande's power. By this time his eldest sons had reached early manhood and were starting to build up personal followings in anticipation of a succession struggle on the king's death. The lack of a clearly designated successor gave a number of powerful territorial chiefs and *izinduna*, who were seeking to undermine the king's position to their own advantage, the opportunity of putting forward their own candidate for the succession in opposition to the king's. It is impossible to say which party took the initiative, but by about 1852 it was becoming clear that the king's preference was for his second-eldest son Mbuyazi, while the most influential chiefs favoured his eldest son Cetshwayo. During the mid-1850s the rivalry between them began breaking out into the open, and by 1856 the nation had split into two camps, with Cetshwayo commanding much the larger degree of support. Mpande has often been blamed for not intervening in the dispute and so preventing civil war, but he could not have resolved the matter without referring it to his councillors. This would have meant playing into the hands of the opposition, who were by far the strongest party. A political solution was impossible without gravely weakening the king's power, so he seems to have been prepared to chance a military confrontation as a means of deciding the issue. He also hoped to secure the intervention on his side of the Natal government.

In the event it was the chiefs who won. In November 1856 Mpande brought the issue to a head by allocating to Mbuyazi and his followers, or iziGqoza as they were known, a tract of country on the Thukela to enable him, it seems, the more easily to try to secure aid from Natal. At once Cetshwayo moved his own following, the uSuthu, to drive them out, and early in December 1856 their two armies met at Ndondakusuka near the Thukela. In a fierce battle the iziGqoza were crushed, and thousands of them—men, women and children—massacred. Mbuyazi and five other sons of Mpande were killed, and the opposition to Cetshwayo was decisively shattered. Mpande's gamble had failed.

'The Man on the Point of a Spear'

After Cetshwayo's victory the way now seemed clear for him to get rid of his father and usurp the kingship, but several factors held him back. Though he was nearly thirty years old he had not yet been granted royal permission to put on the headring and marry, and so was still regarded by the nation as a 'boy'. Without full adult status he could not make any final bid for power without risking the loss of much of his following. Mpande still had considerable, if unorganized, support in the land, and there was in addition the possibility that he could win the intervention on his behalf of either the Boers or the British. The struggle between king and opposition continued, but now on a diplomatic level. Both Mpande and Cetshwayo sent a succession of messengers to the British in Natal to request their intervention, and Cetshwayo made overtures to his father's old allies, the Boers.

Beyond sending a commission of enquiry to investigate Zulu affairs early in 1857, the Natal authorities refused to become involved in the dispute. For their part, the Boers believed that the Sand River Convention of 1852 had given them suzerainty over the Zulu country, but internal dissensions and troubled frontiers made it difficult for them to give full effect to their claims. Nevertheless the flight of Cetshwayo's brother Mthonga to Utrecht in February 1861 provided the Boers with an opportunity to intervene in Zulu affairs. Unbeknown to Mpande, they entered into negotiations with Cetshwayo, and in March concluded an agreement with him in terms of which the Boers handed over Mthonga in exchange for a cession of land on the Zulu kingdom's western border. The Boers also agreed to recognize Cetshwayo as Mpande's successor, while Cetshwayo in turn promised to do his father no harm.

The British acted swiftly to counteract the advantage which the Boers had thus gained. In Cape Town, High Commissioner Wodehouse made clear that the Imperial Government would not allow Boer expansionist plans to go through, and in April 1861 Theophilus Shepstone, Secretary for Native Affairs in Natal, went into the Zulu country formally to proclaim Cetshwayo as Mpande's successor.

Four years after his military victory at Ndondakusuka, Cetshwayo had thus clinched a political victory as well. Henceforth he exercised many of the prerogatives formerly held by Mpande. But the old king remained more than the mere figurehead which he has often been depicted as. He could still rely on the support of the Boers and British in the event of Cetshwayo's planning to remove him, and within his kingdom he remained the ultimate legitimating authority by virtue of the important ceremonial offices that only he could perform. Without his agreement new age-grades could not be formed, existing ones could not marry, and the nation's most important public rituals, such as those connected with the annual *umkhosi* or 'first-fruits' festival, could not be performed. Cetshwayo continued to pay him formal homage as head of state, and to refer certain decisions to him for his stamp of approval. To his people he was still the *inKosi* or king, while Cetshwayo was the *umNtwana* or prince.

Though king and prince continued to manoeuvre against each other after 1861, neither was prepared to go so far as to endanger the existence of the kingdom, which in the last years of Mpande's reign was facing a growing threat from the Boers in the west. Cetshwayo had soon repudiated his land cession of 1861, and thus generated a serious frontier dispute which became the pivot of the subsequent complications in the relations between Natal, the South African Republic, and the Zulu. By 1864 the republic had achieved some measure of internal unity, and in December of that year the Boers asserted their claim to the ceded territory by beaconing it off. Because he needed their support against Cetshwayo, Mpande could not refuse outright to ratify the land cession made by his son, and so adopted a temporizing position towards the republic while sending a series of complaints to the British about Boer conduct. In 1869, after the Boers had taken a number of Zulu under their authority and had begun to exact taxes from them, these complaints culminated in an appeal to the British to arbitrate in the dispute. The South African Republic was prepared to accept the Natal government's consequent offer of arbitration, but no action was taken in Mpande's life-time.

The internal political history of the Zulu kingdom in the 1860s and the nagging frontier dispute with the Boers must be seen against the background of the major economic depression which occurred in the Zulu country in the late 1850s and early 1860s. The military operations at the end of 1856 had dislocated normal life in much of the kingdom, but more serious was the loss of great numbers of cattle in the epidemic of lungsickness which swept over much of south-east Africa in the second half of the 1850s. In the early 1860s a prolonged drought badly affected the people's harvests, causing near-famine in many parts of the country, and in 1864 epidemics of influenza and smallpox killed numbers of people already enfeebled by several years of poor diet. Food shortages were compounded by the steady depletion of the country's game resources which had been carried out since the 1840s by white hunters and their parties of black retainers.

In 1867, prompted by the growing Boer threat in the west, and the knowledge that he was nearing the end of his life, Mpande at last gave permission for Cetshwayo and his age-grade to put on the headring and marry. The king was no doubt well aware that were he to die in troubled times without a 'man' to succeed him, the consequences for the Zulu kingdom could be calami-tous. In making this major political decision he helped ensure that the kingship which he had seized by force, and defended for nearly thirty years, would pass to his heir in orderly fashion. Many years before, the praise-singers had sung of his grandfather Jama, 'Even on the point of a spear he can be at ease'. These words could serve as a fitting epitaph to Mpande's own career.

Conclusion

Mpande died in September or October 1872 and was buried at Nodwengu according to the customs of his people. 'The sons of Senzangakhona are mad bulls,' he had once said, and he was the only one of them to die a peaceful death. In itself this is a tribute to his remarkable ability to survive through an age when southern Africa was undergoing a political and social revolution. But he had done more than simply survive. After seizing the chance which had come his way to make himself head of the most powerful black state in southern Africa, he had manoeuvred successfully to maintain his position for more than three decades, and in doing so had accepted changes in the nature of the Zulu monarchy which, even if they reduced its powers, at least ensured its continuity. When faced with the intransigence of strong subordinates he had had the political sense to bow to the inevitable and accept a limitation of his authority, and so ensure that his successor Cetshwayo inherited an undivided kingdom. Externally, his diplomatic skills had enabled him to maintain peace with the Boers and the British while playing them off against each other to his own advantage.

But Mpande's reign was by no means a story of unqualified success. In failing to curb his subordinate chiefs he had allowed some of them to build up their power to the point where, given the chance, they could challenge the monarchy itself, as Cetshwayo later found to his cost. The factions that had developed during Mpande's reign were key elements in the civil war of 1881–4 which largely destroyed the social and political fabric of Zulu society. In manoeuvring between the British and Boers he had been unable to prevent the development of a border dispute which, after his death, began to threaten the territorial integrity of the Zulu kingdom. And, perhaps most important of all, during his long reign he had allowed the institutions of Zulu society to develop a degree of fixity which would stand the nation in ill stead when, in the later nineteenth century, it was dragged by force into the world of the white men. If the Zulu kingdom was one of the African societies least prepared for coping with the traumatic impact of the changes that followed from the discovery of diamonds and gold in southern Africa, Mpande must share some of the blame for not steering it towards a greater degree of timely adaptation.

But this is to judge with all the advantages of hindsight. In terms of his own times, Mpande was not perhaps the best leader that the Zulu might have had, but he was at least a competent one. In the words of the praises which his people gave him, he was 'the thunder which pounds at the stones and rumbles; the sun which stands alone in the heavens; the elephant which devoured men.'

Further Reading

D. R. Morris, *The Washing of the Spears* (New York, 1965).

Max Gluckman, 'The Kingdom of the Zulu in South Africa' in M. Fortes and E. Evans-Pritchard, eds., *African Political Systems* (London, 1940).

A. T. Bryant, *Olden Times in Zululand and Natal* (London, 1929).

C. de B. Webb and J. Wright, eds., *The James Stuart Archive*, Vol. I (Pietermaritzburg, 1976).

R. Mael, 'The Problems of Political Integration in the Zulu Empire', Ph.D. thesis, University of California, Los Angeles, 1974.

P. Kennedy, 'The Fatal Diplomacy: Sir Theophilus Shepstone and the Zulu Kings, 1839–1879', Ph.D. thesis, University of California, Los Angeles, 1976.

4
Mswati II
c. 1826–65

After Sobhuza I had laid the foundations of the Swazi nation, Mswati II, his son and heir, consolidated his work, suppressing internal resistance and meeting the Zulu challenge, in part by making a tactical alliance with a group of Transvaal Trekkers. In the last decade of his reign he was able to go over to the offensive and expanded his kingdom to the south and north.

For a major southern African leader Mswati remains a remarkably shadowy figure. The careers of Moshoeshoe, Khama, and many other African leaders are documented in a variety of sources, but for Mswati we have only the limited pre-occupations of oral traditions, the bald record of diplomatic intercourse with the Boers, and passing glimpses from two missionary accounts. Only one physical description of Mswati exists—that of the Berlin missionaries Merensky and Grutzner, who visited Mswati in April 1860—which, typically, tells us tantalizingly little. Mswati, we learn,

> *was of kingly appearance, a large man, slightly heavy in body, with a mild expression you would not have expected. He was shaven headed, without* blankets, clad in just the usual majoba of the kaffers, and with an 'ibetsjoe' of expensive skins and tails.*[1]

And that is more or less all.

His personality is even more of a closed book. The records of the South African Republic are uniformly silent on the subject, and we are left with only the stereotypical views of oral and missionary sources which portray him as 'fierce' or 'brave', but as very little else. For all that, two themes can be drawn out of the oral material: his role in the consolidation of the emergent Swazi state, and his remarkably successful military career. Together with the close ties he established with the Boers, which

8 *Mswati*

contributed materially to his success in domestic and military arenas, these provide the basic framework for our present account.

Mswati's reign opened amidst challenges from within and without. Most serious initially were new Zulu attacks. The Swazi had suffered periodic onslaught from this quarter since the rise of Zulu power, the most recent being the invasion of 1836, but these had always had the limited and transitory objectives of seizing booty from the Swazi, and checking the rise of a growing local power. After Dingane's defeat at Blood river in 1838 this previously stable configuration underwent radical change. In terms of the treaty subsequently concluded with the Boers, Dingane agreed to withdraw from territory south of the Black Mfolozi river, and he now sought to compensate for his losses by seizing control of Swazi territory north of the Pongola river. Accordingly, in the summer of 1839, he sent his Mbelebele, Imkulutshane and Nomdayana regiments to build a military village at Lubuya, near the present town of Hlathikhulu, as the first step in his plan.

In the midst of this crisis Mswati came to power on the death of his father. He could hardly have acceded in less favourable circumstances, since Sobhuza's death was bound to affect the army's morale. But the news was kept secret from the army and the regiments went to battle in ignorance of what had occurred. Though Swazi casualties were large, Zulu losses were larger still. According to some accounts more than half of the Zulu regiments were destroyed, and when the Swazi returned to the fray the next day they found the Zulu forces had withdrawn. For the Swazi it was a resounding victory, but the Zulu threat was far from past. Defeat had left Dingane even more implacably determined to seek a final reckoning with the Swazi, and it was not until the rebellion of his half-brother Mpande, and the subsequent defeat of Dingane by the combined forces of Mpande and the Natal Boers, that the Swazi were freed of the prospect of renewed efforts at Zulu colonization.

What part did Mswati play in these events? In all probability it was not very great. Because he was still young, probably only thirteen years old, it seems likely that most decisions of importance were taken by the regents Thandile (his mother), Malunge (his paternal uncle), and Malambule (his eldest brother), who were ruling in his name. Only later, once he had passed through the rites of circumcision in 1845, was Mswati able to assume a

more dominant rôle in Swazi affairs. Even then, no really fundamental changes in the character of Swazi government took
place. Throughout, it continued to function on a conciliar basis,
and it is for this reason that Mswati's achievements deserve
to be remembered as the achievements of his *liqoqo* councillors,
in particular Thandile and Malunge, as much as of Mswati himself.

Internal and External Challenges

Mswati's problems were not simply confined to the Zulu,
although it is probably true to say that the Zulu invasions aggravated every other one of the difficulties with which he was faced.
Equally, if not more serious, was disaffection within the royal
house. Because Mswati had been young when Sobhuza died, a
number of his elder brothers had entertained hopes that they
might be selected as Sobhuza's heir, and even after these hopes
were dashed by Mswati's nomination, some continued their
intrigues. Of these, Fokoti was the least amenable to the young
king's control, and it was he that was the first to raise the banner
of revolt, within months of the Zulu invasion. In this crisis
Mswati again owed much to his regents' loyalty and support,
for while Fokoti succeeded in raising support in southern
Swaziland (his own chiefdom was situated in the vicinity of
modern Mahamba) Malunge saved the day by rallying the regiments at the royal capital, thereby ensuring the revolt would be
quickly suppressed.

Though the rebellion was soon over, the alarm that it created
among the ruling group took longer to subside. What had
happened once could happen again, and it was to forestall this
possibility that the queen mother, Thandile, now embarked
on a programme of internal reform, aimed at consolidating
central authority over Swaziland's disparate chiefdoms and
clans. Thandile's programme was an ambitious one. A system of
nation-wide age regiments was created to replace the older more
localized units of military organization; a more extensive network of royal villages was set up to help co-ordinate military and
political activities; and a series of important innovations were
introduced into the annual *iNcwala* ceremony, to enhance the
ritual authority of the monarchy. It is possible in fact that even
more was attempted than this, as there are indications that the
reform package ran into unexpectedly strong opposition from

Swaziland's regional chiefs, and had to be broken down.[2] But even if the plan that was ultimately adopted was more modest than its prototype, it still proved a major advance on what had gone before, and it was to serve as the basis for royal authority and national solidarity until Swaziland's subjection to colonial rule in 1894.

Fokoti's rebellion, as Thandile suspected, was to be no isolated event, and Mswati's troubles with his brothers continued well into the 1850s. Next to challenge him was the regent Malambule. What drove him to rebellion remains clouded and obscure. Oral traditions claim that the confrontation arose out of a dispute over cattle which Malambule had previously seized from Fokoti, but it seems likely that its roots went deeper than that. A more convincing explanation is suggested by the timing of the clash. The final breakdown of relations between Mswati and Malambule came early in 1846, only a few months after a major re-distribution of political power. In mid-1845 Mswati finally passed through circumcision rites, which now entitled him to the full exercise of royal powers. For Malambule this had meant a corresponding diminution in authority, and this he evidently found unable to accept, expressing his resentment by his refusal to surrender cattle seized from Fokoti. The refusal represented a direct challenge to Mswati's authority, and could only mean one of two things: Malambule had either to flee the country or resist Mswati by arms. Either way the scene was set for open confrontation.

It was not long before it became clear that Malambule's rebellion constituted a far more formidable threat to Mswati than that of Fokoti, a few years before. Malambule possessed all the political advantages of Fokoti, and a few more besides. Like Fokoti he was a prominent son of Sobhuza. Like Fokoti he had control of a chiefdom in the south of Swaziland (near La Vumisa) from which he could mount his revolt. And like Fokoti, he may have been nominated for the succession before Sobhuza's death. What made him so much more dangerous than his brother was the assistance he was able to enlist in his support. First the missionary Allison, and then the Zulu king Mpande, were conscripted to his cause. For Allison, who had founded his Swazi mission at Mahamba only a short while before, the association was a largely unwitting one, although this did not save him from being expelled from Swaziland for his part in these events. Mpande, however, was a more willing ally. For him the rebellion came as a perfect opportunity to pursue his expansionary aims in Swaziland, and, with Malambule as his pretext, Zulu armies once again tramped into Swaziland in January 1847.

How Mswati would have fared had he been compelled to rely solely on his own resources is difficult to say. As it was, however, he had the good fortune to be able to call to his assistance the support of a group of Boer farmers who had only just made their appearance in the area, and with their aid the Zulu armies were expelled from Swaziland in July 1847. Malambule's subsequent history was a brief and unhappy one. After a short stay in Zululand he was denounced by enemies for alleged complicity in the death of Dingane and put to death by Zulu executioners.[3]

The 1846 alliance with the Ohrigstad Boers was to be of lasting importance for the Swazi and ranks among the leading achievements of Mswati's reign. Because of this it is important to understand how it came into being and why it persisted for so long. In part, as we have seen, it arose out of Mswati's need for Boer protection against Zulu attack. But equally if not more important was the Boers' own need of Swazi support. Much of this proceeded from internal divisions within the Boer community. After their arrival in the eastern Transvaal the Ohrigstad Boers had soon become divided into two opposing camps. On the one side there were those who adhered to the Commandant General, Potgieter, on the other those who supported the Volksraad or elected council. Mswati played on this division by offering an alliance to the Volksraaders on terms that would strengthen their internal position against Potgieter. In return for their help against the Zulu they were promised the cession of a huge tract of land in the eastern Transvaal, stretching from the Olifants river in the north to the Crocodile river in the south, and the prospect of Swazi co-operation in the years to come. It was an offer that they could scarcely refuse, and the treaty was signed on 26 July 1846.

Although it is rarely recognized as such, the agreement was a master-stroke of Swazi diplomacy. As a direct result, the Zulu were expelled, and the Swazi acquired at least a partial insurance against future Zulu attack. In return all they surrendered was territory over which they had little control, and only the flimsiest of rights, together with the promise of future support. Yet, as so often happened in these early years of Mswati's reign, triumph over one adversity in itself contained the seeds of another. The next hurdle that presented itself was the secession of

Mswati's brother Somcuba, which arose directly out of the alliance with the Boers. As Sobhuza's eldest son Somcuba enjoyed a special status in Swaziland which had been considerably enhanced by the 1846–7 civil war. During those disturbances he not only led the Swazi armies against Malambule, but also acted as chief negotiator in Mswati's dealings with the Boers. Once the Zulu had been expelled from Swaziland, Somcuba's close association with the Boers proved a growing threat to Mswati, as it came to be employed more and more in the interests of Somcuba rather than in those of the kingdom as a whole. Once this became apparent to Mswati the scene was set for a new bout of civil war. Again the final breakdown in relations came after a dispute over cattle—in this case the cattle received for the 1846 cession, which Somcuba refused to hand over to Mswati. Mswati's answer was to send an armed force against Somcuba, probably late in 1849. Somcuba, however, was prepared for this contingency and had already retired to a cave near the Komati river. Against this Mswati's troops could make little impression and had to return empty-handed shortly after. The first round had therefore gone to Somcuba, but he was not so foolish as to be deluded by this success. He knew that Mswati would soon be returning, this time with a vastly stronger force, so he fled to Boer sanctuary in the eastern Transvaal.

Somcuba found refuge among the Boers for the next six years, during which time Swazi/Boer relations came under considerable strain. The difficulties over Somcuba did not stem just from his flight to Lydenburg. What offended even more was his behaviour once he was there. Three things in particular compounded his offences in Swazi eyes. First was his amalgamation of local Pai and Sotho chiefdoms in the Crocodile river region into a substantial chiefdom. Second, was his harassment of Swazi messengers sent to parley with the Boers. Third, and most serious, was his usurpation of royal perogatives by performing his own *iNcwala* celebration. If ever there was any chance of Mswati's reconciling himself to Somcuba's presence in Lydenburg, this ruled it out. Henceforth his overriding objective was the destruction of Somcuba, whatever the protection he enjoyed. There followed a testing time for the Lydenburg Boers. First, access to Delagoa Bay through Swaziland was shut off (1850); then they saw the Swazi conniving in a Zulu attack on their neighbouring Pedi (1850); and finally they found their own capital at Lydenburg besieged by a Swazi army as a prelude to a new Swazi move against Somcuba (1853). Only in 1855–6 was the basis for normal relations restored, after Mswati's forces had made a spectacular 'human chain' crossing of the flooded Crocodile river, catching Somcuba unawares and causing his death.

The Zulu and Natal

Somcuba's death and a new treaty of cession with the Lydenburg Boers which shortly preceded it in 1855 mark the opening of a new and more expansive era in Mswati's foreign relations. But before looking at that, it is necessary for us to turn our attention back to the period 1850–2, to examine another development which in many ways provided the springboard for this later expansion. Apart from Somcuba, Mswati's chief worry in the early 1850s was with the Zulu. It was a problem which became particularly acute after the secession of Somcuba, for the hostility that this injected into Swazi/Lydenburg relations now ruled out any prospect of Boer aid in the event of any further Zulu attack. The Boers, it is true, were not the only power to whom Mswati could address an appeal for help. The Natal authorities were in a position to help, but the problem here was to persuade them to use the influence they had. Mswati had met with small success in his appeals to Natal at the time of the Zulu invasion of 1846–7, and his new requests during 1850 achieved equally little effect. In reply to a call for assistance in 1850, all the British could do was to suggest he became tributary to the Zulu. To the British the issue was evidently academic. To Mswati it was becoming a matter of life and death. Already in 1849 a Zulu army had made another attack on Swaziland—albeit rather disjointed and inept—and all the signs pointed to still more damaging incursions ahead. Natal's refusal therefore left only one avenue open to Mswati and in 1850 he took it by tendering his submission to the Zulu monarch Mpande.

Mpande accepted Mswati's submission grudgingly and seems never to have intended to keep to its obligations. Indeed his principal object in accepting it seems to have been to lull the Swazi into a false sense of security, with a view to encompassing their total defeat. If that was his plan it succeeded admirably. When the Zulu armies again crossed the Pongola in 1852 the Swazi were taken completely by surprise. Many died, and still more fled, until at one point it looked as if the whole nation might disintegrate. So serious was the situation that Mswati was driven at one point to ask Natal for sanctuary for himself and his people. As a result, when the Zulu armies did finally evacuate Swaziland after a six month occupation, they left behind a shattered, demoralized country, and a people whose capacity to withstand further attacks lay seriously in doubt.

In the event the Swazi were never called upon to put that question to the test, as no further invasions of Swaziland ensued. One reason for this was that Mpande became the victim of his own success. So grim had been the tales of Zulu devastation in Swaziland that the Natal authorities began to fear a massive inflow of refugees into Natal (Mswati in fact may have deliberately exaggerated Swaziland's plight to achieve this effect). To avoid this the Natal government now began to apply pressure on Mpande to abstain from further attacks. Mpande was in no position to resist. With his elder sons reaching maturity in Zululand, his authority was coming under increasing challenge from within, and in the event of future struggle British help could prove decisive. Accordingly, he could not afford to alienate them now, and his armies were ordered to refrain from any further depredations among the Swazi.

For the time being, then, Swazi security was assured. But no one knew better than Mswati that it rested very precariously on the continued benevolence of Natal, and persisting weakness of the Zulu. The second Mswati could do little about; the first, however, he took steps to reinforce. The technique that Mswati adopted was the traditional one of a marriage alliance. At the suggestion of the *liqoqo* councillor Malunge, overtures were made to Sir Theophilus Shepstone, the Secretary for Native Affairs in Natal, for the conclusion of a marriage pact between himself and one of Mswati's sisters. No one of course thought that Shepstone would marry Mswati's sister Tifokati himself. Rather they suggested that the union between the two houses be consummated by proxy, through the medium of Shepstone's chief *indvuna* Ngoza. With that, the object of the manoeuvre would be accomplished. Shepstone would have a personal stake in Swaziland's freedom from Zulu attack, while the friendship between Swaziland and Natal would be brought home to the Zulu in the most emphatic way. At the same time, a source of intelligence would be planted at the heart of the Shepstone camp. It may be wondered nevertheless why the Swazi thought that even this limited proposal might succeed. On the face of it it conferred little benefit on Shepstone, entailing only obligations against the Zulu. Here again, however, the answer seems to be that the Swazi had weighed up their opposite numbers remarkably shrewdly. Throughout this period Shepstone had ambitions to form a 'native confederation' in South-Central Africa under his own personal control, and it was this ambition that the Swazi seem to have played upon in securing a marriage connection; it was their success in this manoeuvre which gave Swaziland at least a partial re-insurance against Zulu attack in the years ahead.

Expansion

Together with continuing tensions within Zululand centring around the rivalry of Mpande and Cetshwayo, this protective attitude on the part of the Natal authorities secured Swaziland from Zulu attack for the rest of Mswati's reign. As a result, from about 1856 until his death in 1865, Mswati was able to initiate a series of campaigns designed to expand Swaziland's territory and enhance her political stature. Among the first of these military expeditions were those directed against the north-east and south-west. From the earliest days of the Zulu and Swazi states there had been a no-mans-land of disputed political authority between the two, and it was this region that Mswati first set his sights on to reconquer. As a result, in the years 1857—8 the chiefdoms of the Magonondo, the Nkhosi Shabalala and the Nhlapo each felt the weight of Mswati's military might in turn. Of the three the Nhlapo proved the most resistant to Swazi arms, victory being denied on one occasion by a freak fall of snow. Nevertheless in 1860, the Nhlapo leader, Mhlangala, was finally vanquished by Mswati and the Nhlapo incorporated within the Swazi state.[4]

At more or less the same time, Mswati was prosecuting a series of campaigns in the north-east. Here Mswati's authority had been seriously undermined by the disruptions of the earlier part of his reign. As a result the Madolo and the Sifundza of Shewula had thrown off royal control. While Shewula was quickly dealt with, the Madolo proved a more obstinate adversary. The difficulty with them was their alliance with the Portuguese, who were trying to extend their authority from the fort at Lourenco Marques. However, with his confidence growing daily, Mswati was not deterred for long, and between 1856 and 1863 a series of invasions was launched against the Madolo and neighbouring areas, which were nominally tributary to the

Portuguese. In the face of these incursions the Portuguese proved helpless to resist and their position was so eroded by the middle of 1863 that Mswati's armies were even able to bottle them up inside the fort.

The Swazi investment of Lourenco Marques was a major display of military might. Nothing like it had been seen since Dingane's attack in 1834, which had led to the execution of the Portuguese Governor. Even so, it was far from being the most spectacular of Mswati's military excursions. This description must go to Mswati's intervention in the Shangane (Gaza Nguni) succession crisis of 1861–2. The Shangane succession crisis erupted in 1861, following a rebellion against the ruling monarch Mawewe by his half-brother Mzila. Mawewe had emerged as a ruler of the Shangane empire after a brief civil war that had followed his father's death three years before. Among the defeated in that conflict was Mzila, who had fled to the Zoutpansberg Boers for asylum. From here he had conspired against his brother with the Zoutpansberg Boers, disaffected elements within the Shangane empire and the Portuguese. In 1861 Mzila's conspiracies came to fruition. After marching to Delagoa Bay, picking up disaffected elements on the way, he combined with the Portuguese and in two battles decisively defeated Mawewe.

It was at this point that Mswati became drawn into the conflict. Mswati was linked to the Shangane royal house through his marriage to two of Mawewe's sisters, and it was to him that Mawewe fled following his defeat. At an earlier stage in his reign Mswati would probably have done no more than to offer Mawewe asylum. Now, however, he was in a position to exploit the dispute and to appropriate the various forms of booty that involvement would bring, in particular the ivory and slaves so much in demand in the Transvaal. Accordingly, two regiments were supplied to Mawewe, and the combined forces marched north to restore Mawewe to the throne.

The intervention was astonishingly successful: Mzila's forces were scattered, and Mzila himself put to flight. At this point however Mawewe overstretched himself. Without consolidating his position, and with Mswati's forces already returning home, he pursued Mzila far into the north. The march proved too much for his battle-weary soldiers, and they fell easy prey to a counter attack by Mzila. The result was that once more Mawewe had to flee south, where in a final battle between 17 and 20 August 1862 he was comprehensively defeated.

Again Mawewe took sanctuary with Mswati and this time he was provided with a chiefdom in the north of Swaziland. It must have been clear to Mswati by now that Mawewe was a lost cause, but this did not mean that he was going to give up his own ambitions in the north. Under threat of Swazi attack Mzila had already been obliged to remove his capital far to the north, which meant that in effect he had abandoned his territory south and west of the Limpopo. Into this vacuum Mswati now moved. Repeated expeditions were sent north in the remaining years of Mswati's life, to loot the area of ivory, cattle and captives, so that by the end of Mswati's reign in August 1865 effective Swazi control stretched to the Sabie river and beyond.[5]

Conclusions

Taken together, then, Mswati's conquests were impressive, and Swazi territories were expanded to a size previously unattained. Viewed against this background the legal definition placed on Swaziland's boundaries by the 1846 and 1855 cessions appear all the more unrealistic and absurd. In the longer term they undoubtedly acquired considerable importance, since on them rested the Transvaal's right to much of its land. For the duration of Mswati's reign however they were of much less significance. To begin with, neither side seems to have had much intention of keeping to their provisions. One of the unwritten conditions of the 1855 treaty, for example, had been that the Transvaalers occupy a strip of territory along the north bank of the Pongola river to act as a shield against Zulu attacks. This they never did (at least until the 1890s) and it is doubtful whether they ever had the slightest intention of doing so. Mswati, for his part, treated his obligations equally lightly. Such use as the treaty had for him derived from the protection it gave against the Zulu; once the Zulu threat receded it is not surprising to find Mswati acting as if the treaty never existed. Probably the best reading of the situation is that throughout the period the interpretation of the treaty was simply a reflection of overall balance of power. In the early 1860s the Transvaal was relatively weak, Swaziland relatively strong. Only when the relative strength of the two sides altered, would the Transvaal be able to impose its own interpretation of Swaziland's treaty obligations.

The earlier part of Mswati's reign, we have noted, was plagued with difficulties with his brothers. These continued, with at least two more brothers (Mgidla and Hhobohhobo) being executed for sedition. Similar tensions were present in his relations with his subordinate chiefdoms. These, it will be recalled, had been strained by the reforms which had followed Fokoti's rebellion, which had generated such a wave of reaction that Mswati had been forced to back down. After the Zulu invasions of 1847 Mswati quietly resumed the same process with measures designed to extend his ritual, political and economic power. The provinces predictably resisted these inroads, with the result that the last decade of Mswati's reign was punctuated by attacks on subordinate chiefdoms, which extinguished the last vestiges of their local autonomies and finally consolidated effective royal power.

What conclusions can we draw about Mswati as a person, and as a king? First of all it seems clear that Mswati's entire personality and view of the world were moulded, and to some extent distorted, by the early experiences of his life. The repeated challenges he experienced from elder brothers in the early part of his reign bred in him an almost morbid suspicion of his associates in power. Still worse, these fears could be played upon by those jockeying for position at court. His body servant, Khambi Sikhondze, was the most notorious of these, and is alleged to have been responsible for many innocent deaths.[6] Nevertheless, Mswati's reign is not characterized in the main by abuses of power. Most of the violence and bloodshed for which he was responsible can be traced to the pressing need to consolidate his power. Similarly, though he was the best placed of Swaziland's kings to emerge as a despot, he never assumed despotic powers, preferring to draw on the wisdom of elder statesmen like Thandile and Malunge in the wider interests of the Swazi aristocracy and state. That the Swazi monarchy survived intact through the colonial era is in some measure a tribute to his success in doing that.

NOTES

[1] T. Wangemann, *Maléo en Sekoekoeni* (Cape Town, 1957), p. 20.

[2] Natal Archives, Garden Papers, file IVB (Swazis), pp. 58–60, 1158, 1167; Swaziland Archives, de S. G. M. Honey, 'A History of Swaziland'.

[3] Natal Archives, Stuart Papers, Ms 29393: statement by Ndukwana.

[4] J. H. Nhlapo, 'The Story of Amanhlapo', *African Studies*, 4 (1945).

[5] G. L. Liesegang, 'Beiträge zur Geshichte des Reiches der Gaza Nguni im südlichen Mocambique

1820—1895', Ph.D. thesis,
Cologne, 1967; A. Grandjean,
'Une page d'Histoire inédite.
L'Invasion des Zoulous dans le
Sud-est Africain', *Bulletin de la
Societé Neuchateloise de Geographie*,
XL (1899).

[6] J. S. M. Matsebula, *Izakhiwo Zama-
Swazi* (Johannesburg, 1953);
A. M. Nxumalo, 'Oral Tradi-
tion Concerning Mswati II',
*Occasional Paper no. 1 of the
School of Education, U.B.L.S.,
Swaziland.*

FURTHER READING

J. S. M. Matsebula, *A History of
Swaziland* (Cape Town, 1972).

Hilda Kuper, *An African Aristocarcy:
Rank among the Swazi* (London,
1947).

T. S. van Rooyen, 'Die Verhouding
tussen die Boere, Engelse, en
Naturelle in die Geskiedenis van
die Oos Transvaal tot 1882',
*Archives Year Book for South
African History*, 1951, Vol. 1.

P. L. Bonner, 'The Rise, Consolidation and Disintegration of
Dlamini Power in Swaziland
between 1820 and 1889. A
Study in the Relationship of
Foreign Affairs to Internal
Political Development', Ph.D.
thesis, University of London,
1977.

5
Cetshwayo kaMpande
c. 1832–84

Cetshwayo established himself as heir during his father Mpande's lifetime, and became Zulu ruler on his death in 1872. His great challenge came seven years later, when British forces invaded his kingdom. With the Zulu defeat, Cetshwayo was exiled at the Cape. Three years later, the British were persuaded to allow him to return to Zululand. His return did not end the civil war raging in that country, however, but intensified it, and Cetshwayo died with his kingdom in ruins.

Cetshwayo, the son of Mpande, was born at his father's Mlambongwenya homestead, probably towards the end of 1832. Mpande, unlike his predecessors, allowed his sons to survive into manhood. His two eldest, Cetshwayo the son of Ngqumbazi of the chiefly line of the Zungu clan, and Mbuyazi, son of Monase, a favourite wife of Mpande, were recruited into the Thulwana regiment when they reached their late teens. In the 1840s and early 1850s Mpande mounted the last of the great Zulu raids and Cetshwayo received his first military experience in a raid against the Swazi. As he reached maturity supporters of the young prince began to gather round him at the Ekubazeni homestead. These Zulu became known as the Usuthu, a name derived from a drinking boast which referred to the prodigious capacity of the huge Suthu cattle raided from the Pedi. At the same time other Zulu began to associate themselves with Mbuyazi, and a rival faction, the Gqoza, was formed. Tension began to develop between the brothers and came to a head when Mbuyazi and his followers attempted to follow their father's example and cross the border into Natal. The Usuthu cut them off at the Thukela and in December 1856, at the battle of Ndondakusuka, killed Mbuyazi, five other sons of Mpande, and a large number of their followers.

9 Cetshwayo

In the years that followed, Cetshwayo consolidated his position and played an increasingly important role in Zulu affairs. He possessed many of the qualities of a successful leader, being shrewd, politically astute, and having a commanding physical presence. John William Colenso, the Bishop of Natal, visited him in 1859 and his impression of the prince was typical of the effect that Cetshwayo had on those who met him. Colenso found him

a fine, handsome young fellow of about twenty-nine or thirty years of age, tall and stout-limbed, but not at all obese, with a very pleasant smile and good-humoured face, and strong deep voice. He drew himself up now and then with an air of dignity; but altogether the impression he made on us all was very agreeable, and our men, one and all, commended him as a pleasing young prince.[1]

By the 1860s both Mpande and Cetshwayo came to the conclusion that, in their dispute with the Boers, they should try and gain the support of the Colony of Natal. Furthermore Cetshwayo decided that his position within the kingdom would be strengthened if his claim to the throne was recognized by Natal. Thus, in 1861, Natal's Secretary for Native Affairs, Theophilus Shepstone, entered Zululand and recognized Cetshwayo as Mpande's successor. When Mpande died in 1872 there were still areas of difficulty within the kingdom, and the threat from the Transvaal was intensifying. Cetshwayo attempted to deal with these problems by once again appealing to Shepstone; this time the Secretary for Native Affairs was asked to formally recognize his succession to the throne and to intervene in the dispute with the Boers. In August 1873, in a ceremony at the royal homestead, Shepstone 'crowned' Cetshwayo king of the Zulu.

Shepstone's motives for becoming involved in Zulu affairs can be understood primarily in terms of the interests of Natal as he perceived them. Firstly, there was the need for security: the establishment of friendly relations between the numerically small white settler community and the powerful African kingdom was obviously desirable. But there were other considerations which sprang from Natal's economic situation and the 'native policy' Shepstone had devised since he had taken office when the colony was established thirty years before. Natal was a poor colony: there was little opportunity for capital accumulation as its exploitable natural resources were limited and much of its land in the possession of speculators. Colonists tended to blame their economic ills on Shepstone's policy, by which 2,000,000 of the colony's 12,000,000 acres were reserved for African occupation. According to his critics the consequence was that the labour the settlers so sorely needed was 'locked up', allowing the Africans to live in idleness on large, potentially productive tracts of land. In fact Shepstone saw more clearly than his critics the danger implicit in any attempt to drive the African off the land into wage-labour as the settlers wished to do. Furthermore the evidence suggests that, by the time Cetshwayo came to the throne in neighbouring Zululand, the economic activity of Natal Africans, both in and beyond the boundaries of the Reserves, was playing a large part in providing the financial underpinning of the colony. Of Natal's African population of perhaps 300,000 about half were living outside the Reserves, on some 5,000,000 acres, to which they had no legal rights, but were having a considerable portion of the surplus they produced working the land removed in taxes and as labour, or rent-paying tenants.

Shepstone was keenly aware of the dangers of this situation. An increase in the black population, or a change in the overall economic situation, could lead to wholesale evictions and a crisis of major proportions. It was this realisation that made him search with so much energy for an 'outlet' for Natal's 'superabundant' African population. And by the 1870s it seemed to him that Zululand was the only territory which might possibly serve as such an outlet. Nevertheless in 1873 any possibility of such a policy succeeding must have seemed remote. Cetshwayo's kingdom was in many ways unique in southern Africa. Although the old raiding areas of the Zulu were now beyond their reach, and the kingdom was virtually surrounded by settler communities, its core was still in Zulu possession and guarded jealously. While most African societies in southern Africa had lost their independence through military conquest, or their economies had been undermined by colonial expansion, the Zulu kingdom had retained much of its political independence and economic self-sufficiency. The kingdom's economy was still based on the production of grain, and the breeding and exchange of cattle. Each homestead in Zululand was economically self-sufficient and sent its young men for prolonged periods of service in the state army. The Zulu army was perhaps 30,000 strong and regarded with fear and resentment by the kingdom's neighbours. The Transvaal border-Boers looked enviously at the winter grazing in Zululand's valleys, and many Natal settlers felt that both Zulu land and Zulu labour would solve the colony's economic difficulties. But neither community was prepared to consider confronting the military strength of the Zulu kingdom.

Although trade with the Zulu had long been a feature of Natal's commercial life, and many Zulu used imported blankets, hoes and household utensils, the manufacture of these articles was not beyond the capability of the Zulu craftsman. Furthermore the Natal trader came to Zululand to obtain cattle—the traditional surplus commodity produced in the kingdom. As a result trade with the colonial world had little fundamental effect on the structure of Zulu society.

Thus, at the age of forty, Cetshwayo came to the throne of an extremely powerful, politically and economically independent African state. He had secured his claim to the kingship and gained external support in his border dispute with the Transvaal. As he called his regiments to his major homestead, Ulundi, for the national 'first-fruits' ceremony at the end of 1873, his achievements had been considerable and he had good reason to be well satisfied with the situation. And yet, within six years, the British army was preparing to invade the Zulu kingdom, and depose him.

The Invasion of the Zulu Kingdom

At the time that Cetshwayo became Zulu king, southern Africa was experiencing the first effects of the economic revolution which in the next generation was to transform the subcontinent. Up to the 1860s economic activity in southern Africa was based on agriculture and stock-raising, with commercial activity centred on the ports. In terms of capitalist development the region was backward, exports insubstantial and communications undeveloped. At the end of the 1860s, however, diamonds were discovered in the interior and by the next decade capitalist development was beginning to affect all parts of southern Africa. Commercial ventures in the colonies began to prosper and local treasuries gained from customs tariffs. There was a growing market for local agricultural produce, and railway lines began to reach out from the ports to the diamond fields. Africans from most parts of southern Africa (but not the Zulu kingdom) made their way to the diamond fields to sell their labour. Many returned home with guns, adding to the white settlers' sense of insecurity. London began to realise that it would be advantageous to break down some of the formal barriers between the different southern African communities and establish the basis for an administrative structure which would reduce inter-commercial rivalry. More effective communication systems could be built up, which would facilitate the movement of goods and labour, and a common defence policy could be adopted. Thus in the mid-1870s a 'confederation policy' was initiated from London with the intention of creating a strong, united, white-dominated southern Africa, more suited to the demands of expanding capitalist development and able to carry most of its own administrative and military costs, thereby reducing the responsibilities of the British government. Natal was persuaded to accept the plan but the Transvaal posed a problem. However, the Afrikaner republic was economically vulnerable and was having difficulty in subduing its African population. The Colonial Office decided that the man best able to deal with the Transvaal was Shepstone. In April 1877 the newly-knighted, ex-Secretary for Native Affairs for Natal, annexed the Transvaal to Britain and became its first administrator. Desperately in need of Boer support for the annexation, Shepstone travelled to the Zulu border in October 1877 to discuss the boundary dispute with the Zulu and to attempt to use his personal influence to persuade them to accept Boer claims to land within the kingdom. The Zulu councillors who met him at Blood river perceived immediately what had happened and accused him of deserting his ally, Cetshwayo, and going over to the Boers. Shepstone, so used to being treated with the deference due to an infallible Great White Chief, felt that the Zulu accusations were a personal insult, and left the meeting in a fury.

By this time Sir Bartle Frere had been appointed High Commissioner in southern Africa. It was intended that he should crown a long and distinguished career in the imperial service by bringing about confederation. It was soon apparent to him that the Zulu kingdom, powerful, beyond the reach of the forces of capitalism, and feared by its neighbours, was the most immediate obstacle to any such plans. In a long series of despatches he tried to persuade the Colonial Office of the danger posed to southern Africa by the Zulu. In Cetshwayo, Frere discerned a new Shaka, the leader of all those in the region who resisted Christianity and civilization, and wanted to perpetuate the 'idle, sensuous elysium of Kaffirdom'. In the case he tried to build up against the Zulu, Frere drew on information provided by embittered missionaries, and colonists and officials. Frere's most important informant and supporter was Sir Theophilus Shepstone.

After his meeting with the Zulu in October 1877 Shepstone, in the words of a Colonial Office official, 'turned his coat in the most shameless manner'.[2] Thus in the border dispute between the Zulu and the Transvaal he discovered 'the most incontrovertible, overwhelming and clear' evidence, of which he had been previously unaware (and historians have still to discover), that the Boer claims to Zulu land were substantially valid. And in January 1878 Shepstone wrote at length of the threat that the continued existence of Cetshwayo's rule held for white southern Africa:

> *Had Cetshwayo's thirty thousand warriors been in time changed to labourers working for wages, Zululand could have been a prosperous peaceful country instead of what it now is, a source of perpetual danger to itself and its neighbours.*[3]

Faced with the collapse of his diplomatic arrangements Cetshwayo attempted to find new allies amongst the officials, and also took what defensive action he could. The Zulu had over the past few years obtained firearms through the agency of John Dunn, a white trader who acted as secretary and adviser to the king, and who lived the life of a Zulu chief in the kingdom. But by the end of the decade the Zulu had realized that these antiquated trade guns were difficult to maintain and of limited effectiveness. The king built a new homestead in broken country and called it Mayizekanye—translated at the time as 'Let them come'. And when Sir Henry Bulwer, the Lieutenant-Governor of Natal, proposed that a Boundary Commission be appointed to investigate the dispute between the Boers and the Zulu, Cetshwayo gave it his support.

In June 1878 the Boundary Commission presented its findings but, because the report gave support to the position taken by the Zulu, Frere did not publish it. Instead he continued to attack Cetshwayo and his rule in the despatches he sent to England, interpreted minor border incidents as acts of wanton Zulu aggression demanding severe action, and moved troops into Natal.

Towards the end of October 1878 Cetshwayo protested in these terms:

> *What have I done or said to the Great House of England, which placed my father, Panda, over the Zulu Nation, and after his death put me in power? What have I done to the Great White Chief? I hear from all parts that the soldiers are around me, and the Zulu Nation ask me this day what I have said to the white people. . . .*
>
> *The English Chiefs are speaking. They have always told me that a kraal of blood cannot stand, and I wish to sit quietly, according to their orders, to cultivate the land. I do not know anything about war, and want the Great Chiefs to send me the rain. . . .*[4]

But Frere and his supporters were determined to remove this obstacle to a united, white-dominated, progressive southern Africa. They were encouraged by Shepstone's prognostication that the kingdom was deeply divided and that once 'touched' it would 'fall to pieces'. In December 1878, without waiting for formal authority from London, Frere presented a Zulu deputation from Cetshwayo with an Ultimatum which demanded, amongst other things, that the Zulu military system be abolished within thirty days. The king could not carry out such a demand, and Frere knew it. As the Zulu officials who received the Ultimatum said, the abolishment of the military system would

> *lower the country to the debased level of amaKafula [Africans in Natal] . . . therefore they will fight rather than give in on those points.*[5]

In January 1879 three British columns, supported by colonial forces, entered Zululand to enforce the terms of the Ultimatum. Cetshwayo sent the Zulu army against the central column, which was camped at Isandlwana. Although the commanders of the Zulu force had orders to parley with their counterparts, British scouts blundered on the Zulu force and provoked an attack. In one of the greatest defeats in the history of Britain's colonial wars, the camp at Isandlwana was virtually annihilated. Natal lay open to attack by the Zulu but Cetshwayo did not press the advantage he had gained. He still hoped that he could negotiate a settlement on the premise that he was not the aggressor and that he had been invaded without just cause. Furthermore he fully realized that, even if he won immediate military victories, he was fighting an immensely powerful force which would ultimately defeat him. He therefore continued to fight a defensive war; to use his own metaphor, his approach was that of a 'man warding off a falling tree'.

But even a defensive war cost the king and his people dearly. At the victory at Isandlwana the Zulu lost perhaps two thousand men. Moreover to keep the Zulu army mobilized within the kingdom's borders placed a severe strain on the country's economy. Traditionally the Zulu were raiders and the army's main source of supply came from the plundered property of the enemy. In 1879 however the Zulu were fighting on their own soil. Where possible, food stores and cattle had been moved from areas through which the army passed and Zulu troops found it difficult to maintain themselves and suffered severely from hunger.

This failure to develop an effective support system made it impossible for Cetshwayo to carry out the tactics upon which he had decided at the start of the invasion. Well aware of the losses he would sustain if his troops charged over open ground into the volleys from British rifles, and rocket, gatling and artillery fire, he ordered the Zulu not to attack the invaders if they had taken up a defensive position. Instead he wanted them to adopt harassing tactics, to disrupt supply lines, and lay siege to their encampments. But, driven by hunger, the Zulu ignored their commanders, attacked impetuously, and were cut down with huge losses, while the survivors dispersed to their homes. Thus when the Zulu attacked the northern column in March at Khambula, many were starving by the time they reached the British position, and they disobeyed their commander's orders to wait for flanking columns, and attacked, arguing that they had done so at Isandlwana and won. They suffered terrible losses and

When the King heard of the lost battle he was exceedingly angry, and asked, 'Who had given the word for his people to be allowed to fight against Whites who had already entrenched themselves, since even in the open field one Whiteman was nearly as good as ten Zulus? '. . . . For the King's plan had always been, whenever the Whites should have entrenched themselves, to make his army pass by them, in order thus to bring the Whites into the open field, or else to surround them from a distance, and make them die of hunger. But his people had not patience for all this; and, each time they fought, they must go and rest again for two or three months before beginning another fight.[6]

By May 1879 Lord Chelmsford, commander of the British forces, had been able to reinforce and reorganize his troops and entered Zululand once again, this time moving cautiously, scouting with great care, and making sure his positions were well defended. On 4 July, his supply line stretched to the limit, Chelmsford marched a huge square on to the Mahlabathini plain where the royal homestead stood. The Zulu attacked, half-heartedly according to some, were driven off, and the cavalry was released from the square to disperse the force. Chelmsford burnt Ulundi, and then withdrew hurriedly into Natal and resigned his command. Much has been made of the battle of Ulundi: it is seen as the event which restored honour to British arms after the 'humiliation' of Isandlwana and which finally destroyed the power of the House of Shaka. But the many writers on the Zulu war have been so enraptured by the adventure, the 'glamour and tragedy', they see in this brutal attack on an independent African kingdom, that they have been misled by contemporary accounts which exaggerated the significance of Ulundi in order to save military and political reputations.

By July 1879 both sides desperately wanted to end the conflict. In Britain the Conservatives were under attack for initiating an adventurous, costly, and unsuccessful policy in southern Africa. Chelmsford's ability as a military leader was doubted, and Frere had not only acted without due authority, but had seriously misjudged the situation and led Britain into an expensive, politically embarrassing war. After Isandlwana the confederation policy was set aside, and in May both Frere and Chelmsford were superseded by Sir Garnet Wolseley. Wolseley had orders to bring about peace 'with honour', but to avoid any arrangement with the Zulu which would give Britain responsibility for the future government of the country.

Wolseley, who arrived in Zululand a few days after Ulundi, allowed the soldiers and politicians to elevate it to the rank of a decisive military victory and therefore save the shreds of their military reputations; the politicians accepted this as it gave their policy in Zululand a semblance of continuity. Wolseley then put an end to the conflict by announcing that the war had been made against the Zulu king and not the Zulu people, and if the Zulu laid down their arms and returned to their homes they would be left in possession of their land and their cattle. Most Zulu accepted Wolseley's offer. By July 1879 the Zulu realized that some form of settlement would have to be reached with the invaders if they were to be able to resume agricultural production, upon which the society's survival depended. For the economy could not sustain the presence of British troops on Zulu soil much longer. The Zulu people had been under arms for six months, many had lost their grain-stocks and their cattle, and to forgo planting for a season was to risk starvation and social disintegration. Wolseley's announcement, which was completely in accord with the wishes of the British government, gave the Zulu the chance to regain access to their means of subsistence.

The price the Zulu had to pay for this was the dismantling of their centralized political system and the sacrifice of their king. Nonetheless it took nearly two months for the British to capture Cetshwayo. In the thickly-wooded bush north of the Black Mfolozi Cetshwayo was passed from homestead to homestead to avoid the British soldiers hunting for him. When bribery failed, torture eventually revealed the king's whereabouts. At the end of August the Zulu king was captured and, in the company of a few attendants, marched hurriedly to the coast from where he was transported to Cape Town and detained in the Castle there.

On 1 September Wolseley announced the details of his 'settlement' of Zululand. The rule of the Zulu royal house, with its political and military system, was declared to be at an end. The country was divided into thirteen independent chiefdoms, representing, in theory but not in fact, the pre-Shakan chiefdoms whose members it was alleged had suffered so long under the Zulu tyranny. A British Resident, without authority, would serve as the 'eyes and ears' of the British government.

Thus the Zulu had to accept the dismantling of the traditional order and the exile of their ruler. Yet it must not be forgotten that the vigour of their resistance had been a major factor in the abandonment of the policy which sought to force them into a white-dominated federation, and that they remained in possession of most of their land. Moreover the political hierarchy through whom the king ruled survived the war virtually intact. Indeed the leading members of the old order were to play an important part in persuading the British to abandon Wolseley's settlement within three years and in securing the return of Cetshwayo to Zululand. However in doing so they provoked such an intense reaction from within and beyond the borders of Zululand that by 1883 the material strength of the nation had been destroyed in civil war, and Zululand, and its people, lay open to appropriation and exploitation.

Exile, Restoration and Death

The story of Cetshwayo's exile and eventual return to Zululand is an absorbing and tragic one. From his place of detention, on the southernmost tip of Africa, Cetshwayo successfully made contact with sympathizers in Britain, Natal and Zululand. Together they launched a campaign which eventually convinced the British that Cetshwayo still had a role to play in the politics of Zululand.

Much of the success that Cetshwayo and his supporters achieved was the result of the king's personal talents of persuasion and diplomacy. Frere's despatches at the time of the invasion, and the imaginations of the illustrators of popular magazines, had conjured up in the public mind a picture of the Zulu king as a gorilla-like monster. It was a great surprise therefore when it was discovered that he was a 'fine, tall dignified-looking man', and by the time he had reached Cape Town his imposing manner had been commented upon widely. From the start he had objected to being regarded as a curiosity and insisted upon being treated with the deference due to a head of state. He was to use his kingly bearing to great effect. Although he had never been outside his kingdom, could not speak English, and was illiterate, he was politically astute, an intelligent judge of character, and had great personal charm. The tragedy which had overtaken him, the eloquent way in which he protested to visiting dignitaries or journalists against the way in which he had been treated, gained him an increasing number of supporters in influential positions. Whenever possible, in his conversations, letters, and petitions he made known his conviction that he had been unjustly attacked by the nation with which he and his forebears had had the friendliest of relations, and expressed the hope that something would be done to rectify this.

The most active and effective of Cetshwayo's supporters was J. W. Colenso, Bishop of Natal, who had been appalled at the duplicity Frere and Shepstone had shown in their campaign to bring about the invasion of Zululand. After Isandlwana, when colonial antagonism towards the Zulu was at its height, he had used his pulpit in Natal to analyse the political background to the war, and expose the injustice of the invasion. He

10 Zulu in war attire ▶

then reminded his congregation that, while they mourned their dead, as Christians they should not forget those in Zululand who mourned theirs. After Cetshwayo's exile he sent the king the following telegram:

'Sobantu salutes Cetshwayo; he is grieved for him; he does not forget him.'

To which the king replied:

'Cetshwayo thanks Sobantu for this message, and is glad to hear that he does not forget him. He hopes Sobantu will speak well for him.'[7]

Colenso was to exceed all Cetshwayo's expectations. Until his death a few years later Colenso was to work energetically, keeping the king's name in the public eye, gathering support, giving him advice when he could, and serving as an intermediary between Cetshwayo and his allies both in southern Africa and England.

In April 1880 the Conservative government fell and the Liberals under Gladstone came to power. The forward policy of the Conservatives was soon changed to one of retrenchment in southern Africa. Colenso was convinced that the Liberals would do something to 'rectify the past' for, during the election campaign, Gladstone had made much of the British attack on the Zulu, whose 'only offence was their attempt to defend against your artillery with naked bodies their hearths and homes, their wives and families....' Cetshwayo sent a new series of letters to English officials asking to be pardoned. However the Liberal government, while regretting the king's detention, felt that little could be done and that Wolseley's settlement had to be given a chance to prove itself. In November 1880 Colenso visited Cetshwayo in Cape Town and suggested that he ask to be allowed to travel to England to make his appeal personally. At the same time arrangements were made whereby Cetshwayo could contact his followers in Zululand. And a short time later Cetshwayo received an added advantage when R. C. A. Samuelson was appointed as his interpreter.

Samuelson was a missionary's son who had grown up in Zululand and had just completed his education in the Cape. A friendship developed between the young man and the king, and Samuelson was soon passing clandestine messages to Colenso from the king for transmission to Zululand. They passed the weary hours of exile by composing letters, petitions, and a history of the origins of the war as Cetshwayo saw them. These documents had a considerable effect on the men who received them in Downing Street.

Both Gladstone and Lord Kimberley, the Secretary of State for the Colonies, found the letters they received 'painful' but felt, at first, that little could be done for the king. Cetshwayo, depressed, and worried about the news of violence in Zululand, redoubled his efforts. As he expressed it, these letters 'were now his only assegais'. Reports were received from Cape Town that the king might commit suicide. In July 1881 Cetshwayo asked Kimberley,

> *Do you kill me like this because I am a black man?. . . . who could be a greater friend of the English than I, who remained quiet in my country till I was attacked and taken captive. . . . I request you to look to my case and not to my colour, and not leave me to die here while my family is being scattered and is dying off on the hills.*[8]

Worried by the possible scandal if the king killed himself and genuinely affected by his letters, the officials began to consider whether something could be done for Cetshwayo. The opportunity arose when, at the end of 1881, news was received from Zululand of increasing violence in the northern districts. It seemed as if Wolseley's settlement was breaking down, and that a fresh policy towards Zululand would have to be devised. It was suggested that Cetshwayo might play a part in the new arrangements. Meanwhile it was felt that he should be distracted from morbid introspection and allowed to visit England.

The violence which broke out in northern Zululand at the end of 1881 had its origins in the rivalries which developed soon after Wolseley had announced the terms of the settlement of Zululand in 1879. Wolseley's arrangement was a hurried and ignorant one, designed to answer the particular problems facing his political masters at the time. Its basic weakness was not so much that it failed to establish 'effective authority' (as was argued at the time by critics of the settlement, and later by historians), but that it failed to recognize that the war had not fundamentally altered the distribution of power in Zululand. Although the king had been exiled, new authorities created, and high-sounding pronouncements made about the end of the Zulu system, the *izikhulu* (great men) of the nation, and members of the royal family, had survived the war with large followings and substantial material power. Thus, understandably, in those few areas where Wolseley's appo ited chiefs attempted to assert their authority they met with resistance led by representatives of the old order.

Some of the appointed chiefs were nonentities and unable to interfere with existing relations of authority within their chiefdoms; others were sufficiently sensible to avoid doing so. Two of them however, Zibhebhu and Hamu, did impose their new authority, and aided by Wolseley's highly irresponsible injunction that the appointed chiefs collect all royal cattle in their territories, they provoked a civil war.

It is noteworthy that, unlike the vast majority of Zulu, both Zibhebhu and Hamu had close connections with neighbouring white communities. Hamu had received his chiefdom as a reward for being the only Zulu of note to defect to the British during the war. He had a reputation for gratuitous cruelty, was addicted to European spirits, and had living with him a white trader who exploited the timber resources of the nearby Ngome forest. The territory awarded him in 1879 contained some of Cetshwayo's most important supporters including the Qulusi royal section, and the Buthelezi of Mnyamana, who had been the king's chief minister and was the most powerful man in Zululand outside the royal house. On taking up his appointment after the war, Hamu immediately began to take revenge for the losses he had suffered as a result of his defection, and carried out with vigour Wolseley's orders to collect royal property, and harassed and fined many of the Buthelezi and Qulusi. Zibhebhu was awarded a chiefdom in the north-east of the country, bordering on Hamu's, in which were situated many of Cetshwayo's personal homesteads, and those of his close relatives including that of Ndabuko, the king's full brother and guardian to his son Dinuzulu. Zibhebhu had long been known for his energetic trading activities and commercial links with the Colony of Natal. After the war he moved quickly to gather royal property and re-establish his commercial connections. Members of the royal house and their supporters lost cattle they considered their own, and they were fined for allegedly concealing royal property.

Zibhebhu's trading partner was John Dunn. During the war he had deserted his friend and patron, Cetshwayo, and had been awarded a huge territory in the southern portion of Zululand by Wolseley. Dunn collected royal cattle after the war, including some of the best-known herds, handed them over to the British and then bought them back again. He re-established trading links with Zibhebhu, and one of his white associates helped Zibhebhu arm and train a mounted squadron of Zulu. It seemed to many that Zibhebhu and Dunn had entered into a conspiracy to appropriate for themselves the property of the Zulu royal house.

Early in 1880 the British Resident in Zululand and the Natal authorities in Pietermaritzburg received complaints from Mnyamana and Ndabuko that Hamu and Zibhebhu were oppressing them and their followers, seizing cattle unjustly and fining those who were unfortunate enough to be placed under them by the settlement. Melmoth Osborn, the British Resident, obtained permission to inquire into the differences between the parties, on the grounds that if these disputes were not resolved they might lead to violence which could threaten the security of the whole region. However Osborn's interference at this stage did provoke violence and significantly contributed to the outbreak of civil war. He was a close friend of Theophilus Shepstone, who was now living in retirement in Pietermaritzburg after the collapse of the confederation policy and the retrocession of the Transvaal. Although not in office and under something of a shadow, Shepstone's reputation as an expert on 'native affairs' was still high and none of the British officials felt that they could act on important issues in this field without reference to him. Furthermore, Shepstone had relatives and friends in many of the most important posts in the colonial administration. He was therefore able to impose his personal views on official policy towards Zululand in a manner which was to be crucial to the developments of events in that country.

Like Shepstone, Osborn was highly critical of the 1879 settlement. Both felt that some form of colonial overrule should have been instituted. Osborn concentrated on trying to obtain formal authority for the British Resident to take an active role in the administration of Zululand. Shepstone argued that the interests of Natal and Zululand were inseparable and that no policy should be devised for Zululand which did not take Natal's needs into consideration, in particular the urgent problems posed by the need for land for Natal's African population. Both men were totally opposed to any move which might lead to Cetshwayo's return: inadequate as the settlement was it did keep the Zulu politically divided, and excluded Cetshwayo's supporters from authority. The return of the king, they argued, would not only damage the prestige of the white man in the eyes of all Africans, but lead to a revival of the old Zulu system, thereby negating all that had been achieved by the 1879 war.

Thus when, in August 1881, Osborn publicly announced the results of his investigation into the disputes between the appointed chiefs Hamu and Zibhebhu, and Ndabuko and Mnyamana, he came out in favour of the former group. This public demonstration of support by the authorities for the appointed chiefs only encouraged Hamu and Zibhebhu to intensify their harassment of those who had protested against their rule. Ndabuko and his supporters were driven from their homes in Zibhebhu's territory. Hamu attacked the Qulusi royalists and at the beginning of October killed over one thousand of them.

The result was that the Usuthu faction emerged once again as an active force in Zululand. It was led by men like Mnyamana and Ndabuko who had held positions of authority under Cetshwayo, but had lost them in 1879, and who considered that they had been unjustly treated by the chiefs appointed over them. When they had appealed to the representative of the conquering power his mediation had resulted in an intensification of their persecution. They now decided to work actively for the return of Cetshwayo in the hope that this would lead to the re-establishment of the old order in some form. And in doing so they attracted to their side large numbers of Zulu who had lost their positions by the settlement, and now saw a chance of regaining them.

By the end of 1881 the king and Bishop Colenso had worked hard to prepare the way for such an eventuality. Cetshwayo's emissaries from Cape Town had reported publicly on the king's situation, his hopes to return, and the sympathy with which his petitions were being received. The news that Cetshwayo was to go to England reached Zululand in September 1881 and gave his supporters increased confidence, and added to their numbers. At the end of 1881, Colenso transmitted a secret message from Cetshwayo to the leaders of the Zulu telling them to demonstrate publicly for the king's return in order to blunt the effect of official reports of Zulu opposition to Cetshwayo. In April 1882, two thousand Zulu, over six hundred of them men of authority, arrived in Natal to ask for the return of Cetshwayo. The Usuthu faction, born thirty years before to support Cetshwayo's bid for the Zulu throne, was now operating as a pressure-group in the context of colonial and imperial politics.

The Natal officials did what they could to offset the effect of the

Usuthu campaign and alter the direction British policy appeared to be taking. Sir Henry Bulwer began a second term of office as Governor of Natal at the beginning of 1882. Backed by Osborn and Shepstone he opposed the idea that Cetshwayo should be returned, arguing that such an action would retard civilization and progress in southern Africa, and deny Natal the land and labour it so urgently needed. But London insisted that he apply himself to the question, not of whether, but in what manner, Cetshwayo should be returned. These differences in attitude towards Zululand between the metropolitan government, and colonial Natal, were based on differences in their immediate interests. If Natal was to acquire Zulu land and labour she had to ensure that the country remained politically divided; Cetshwayo, it was feared, had the power to unite the Zulu once again. But Britain's policy towards southern Africa, at this time so soon after the disastrous consequences of pursuing confederation, was based on retrenchment and informal control. Her aim was to reduce direct responsibility where she could, and to maintain her dominance by ensuring that the Afrikaner remained confined to the interior of the subcontinent. Thus, in Britain's eyes, the prime function of the Zulu was to block the Transvaal from the coast. However, with the 1879 settlement breaking down, and increasing violence in the northern districts which bordered on the Transvaal, which now had had its independence restored, it seemed as if Zululand would not be able to fulfil this function much longer. Handling the territory over to Natal offered no solution as Britain was ultimately responsible for the colony's defence and security, and she had no confidence in Natal's wisdom or temperance in the field of African administration. Thus, from London's viewpoint, the best plan appeared to be to return Cetshwayo to rule the Zulu. He seemed to be an astute leader, capable of re-establishing a stable, independent, African government which would stand between the Transvaal and the sea. Britain would not be directly responsible for the territory and yet it was believed that she would have considerable informal influence over the king.

This difference in approach to Zulu affairs had a crucial bearing on the development of events in the country. The Natal officials gave support to the appointed chiefs in their opposition to the Usuthu. The Zulu royalists however were encouraged by Britain's favourable attitude towards the king. Thus the factions within Zululand reflected to an important degree divisions beyond the country's borders. Throughout 1882 sporadic violence occured between these factions; violence which, on Cetshwayo's arrival, was to lead to widespread fighting and civil war.

In July 1882 Cetshwayo and his party of advisers and inter-preters arrived in London for discussions on the future of Zulu-land. Cetshwayo's public behaviour was impeccable; he charmed the dignitaries he met, responded with due amazement to the sights he was shown, and was mobbed in the streets by enthusias-tic crowds. Privately he brooded over his future and, fearing assassination, kept to his rooms when he could. Three interviews were held with officials in the Colonial Office. Their usefulness was limited by the fact that Bulwer had still not despatched his detailed report on the future of Zululand. A telegraphic demand had finally forced the Special Commissioner to submit a re-commendation in which he asserted that Cetshwayo could return to Zululand only if a portion of the country, large enough to accommodate all Zulu who opposed him, was alienated from his rule. Cetshwayo objected to this as vehemently as he could under the circumstances and asked to be told the size of the territory which was to be removed. This information Kimberley was unable to give him as Bulwer's detailed recommendations had yet to reach England. However Cetshwayo could not be kept indefinitely in London, and he left in September 1882, pledging allegiance to Britain, but asking that the decision to alienate land from his control be reconsidered.

While Cetshwayo was on his way back to Cape Town, Bulwer's long-awaited despatch on Zululand's future reached the Colonial Office. In it he proposed that the country be partitioned: Zibhebhu should be left independent in the north, the southern districts should be reserved for Zulu not wishing to come under Cetshwayo, and the king should be placed over a portion of land in the centre of the country. London objected to details of Bulwer's plan, but in its broad conception the partition of Zululand, as suggested by the Natal officials, was accepted. Although the officials in the Colonial Office realized that there were fundamental differences between what they had intended, and the proposals put forward by Natal, it was finally decided that, in the face of such intransigence it could not oppose the local officials, who were experts on native affairs, and the very men who would have to implement British policy.

In Cape Town a shocked Cetshwayo was told of the plans and asked to formally agree to them. At first he refused, but threatened

CETSHWAYO kaMPANDE *c.*1832–84

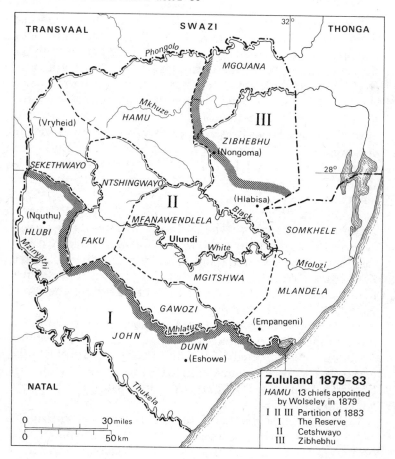

Zululand 1879–83

HAMU 13 chiefs appointed by Wolseley in 1879
I II III Partition of 1883
I — The Reserve
II — Cetshwayo
III — Zibhebhu

with not being allowed to return to Zululand, signed under protest. In January 1883 he landed on the Zululand coast. Sir Theophilus Shepstone's vicious and corrupt brother, John, was already acting as if the district was another Natal native reserve and demanding 'allegiance' from the Zulu under threat of expulsion. Zibhebhu was independent in the north. At the installation ceremony the Usuthu formally protested at the arrangements which had been made, pointing out forcibly that the alienation of the land of the Zulu nation, and the splitting up of kinship and political groups, must lead to violence, and publicly accused Shepstone of plotting to kill the King.

Cetshwayo adopted a policy of vehemently protesting to London about the terms of his restoration, pointing out the difference between what he had been led to believe in England, and the terms finally decided upon. In a series of official messages, and private letters passed on by Colenso, he attempted to rally the men and women he had met during his exile and who had appeared to be on his side. His followers in Zululand however did not find these tactics sufficient. Since the war they had suffered insult and material loss at the hands of Hamu and Zibhebhu, and they now desired revenge. Soon after Cetshwayo's arrival there were violent clashes in different parts of the country between the Usuthu and their enemies. The Natal reports put the blame firmly on Cetshwayo, but as the king himself said, 'I did not land on a dry place. I landed in the mud.'[9]

In March Zibhebhu moved some of his men to evict a group of Usuthu from his territory. The Usuthu from the northern districts decided to put a stop to this once and for all. Probably without the king's permission a huge force was mobilized, entered Zibhebhu's territory, and moved slowly towards his residence burning homesteads as it went. In the broken terrain of the Msebe valley Zibhebhu laid an ambush and on the morning of 30 March took the Usuthu force by surprise. As the foot-soldiers confronted the traditionally-organized and armed Usuthu, Zibhebhu's mounted men supported them with rifle-fire. The Usuthu broke and were cut down as they attempted to flee across the plain that lies east of Nongoma. It is believed that in no battle in Zulu history were more lives lost.

Hamu and Zibhebhu then devastated all Zululand north of the Black Mfolozi driving the Usuthu into the forests and mountains, or into neighbouring territories. For the colonists Zibhebhu had become the 'Napoleon of North Zululand', who was 'really fighting the battle of South Africa, and championing the cause of civilization and order, in the stubborn and so far successful resistance he has offered to the hostility and intrigues of Cetshwayo.'[10] Cetshwayo now openly supported a violent campaign against Zibhebhu and Hamu. He used his influence to gain allies from beyond Zibhebhu's borders while the Usuthu, from their strongholds, harassed Zibhebhu's supporters. By mid-winter a stalemate had been reached, but both sides knew that something had to be done to break the deadlock before the arrival of the spring rains and the planting season. It was Zibhebhu who took the initiative: on the night of 20 July he marched his men towards the royal homestead and at first light launched an attack on Ulundi.

At the time Cetshwayo had residing with him most of Zulu-land's great men. They were old, and, when the Usuthu force failed to hold back Zibhebhu's men, most of the Zulu leaders were killed. The king escaped on horseback but was overtaken on the banks of the White Mfolozi and wounded by a group of Zibhebhu's followers. Cetshwayo turned on his assailants and identified himself, asking how they dared attack their king. Aghast, the men withdrew, and Cetshwayo and a few followers were left to make their way slowly towards the great forest of the Nkandla, the last retreat of so many Zulu in the course of their history. Here the Usuthu survivors built Cetshwayo a hide-out, while Zibhebhu's forces swept northern Zululand once again.

This attack on Ulundi on 21 July 1883 marks the end of the Zulu kingdom. It was not so much the magnitude of the slaughter, although that was terrible enough, but the number of Zulu leaders who supported the king who were killed, which destroyed any chance the Usuthu might have had of regrouping and consolidating their power on a national basis. As Cetshwayo said to a visitor to the Nkandla, after he had given the names of over fifty men killed in the battle:

> *every name I have given you is that of a man of influence, a man with a following; men who say let it be so, Zulu, and it is so in accordance. Ah! but they are gone, and I feel alone. They were men, many my seniors, and favourites of Mpanda, my father, and many of my own age who had grown up with me, belonging to the same regiment, and our life in boyhood and manhood had been one. But they are not. They have been finished. 'Count my headmen who have been killed?' asked the King. 'Easier far to count those who have escaped — the few who are still left to me — left with me to hold our mouths in wonder at the way our own Zulu (nation) is being spilt.*[11]

Zibhebhu now dominated the whole of northern Zululand and sent threatening messages to Cetshwayo. Britain refused to become involved in the confusion, which seemed to bear out Natal's warning that if Cetshwayo was returned he would plunge Zululand into bloodshed. In October 1883 he was persuaded to place himself under Osborn's protection at Eshowe, the Zulu Reserve's administrative centre. It was a dark and despairing time for the king. Colenso had died, exhausted and bitterly disappointed. Cetshwayo continued his appeals to London asking for reinstatement but Britain ignored him. On 8 February 1884 he was found dead in his hut. A cursory medical examination found that he had died of a heart attack, but it was widely believed that he was poisoned. The available evidence remains inconclusive, but, regardless of whether he died as a result of the physical hardship he suffered during his flight and life as a refugee, or whether he was assassinated, in broad terms the responsibility for Cetshwayo's death lay with the men in London who devised his return, and those in Natal who attempted to manipulate the situation in the colony's interests.

Zulu have identified the death of the king with the destruction of the nation, expressing it in the saying '*Kwafa inyoni enkulu kwabola amaqanda*' — 'When the great bird died the eggs became rotten'.[12] With thousands dead or in hiding, and others having lost their food-stores and denied access to arable land, the material power of the Zulu was broken, leaving the country open to external forces. Natal retained its informal hold on the Zulu Reserve. The surviving Usuthu, facing starvation and extinction, called in Boer fire-power to defeat Zibhebhu. This they achieved in 1884 but were then unable to dislodge the Boers who marked out farms from the Transvaal to the sea. Britain decided that it was time to act and the country was partitioned once again, this time, in 1887, between the British and the Afrikaners. Thus in the space of eight years the people of the Zulu nation had lost their land to white farmers, or had come under colonial rule. Zulu labour, so recently expended within the kingdom, was now being exploited on farms and mines beyond Zululand's borders.

Cetshwayo's failure to preserve the kingdom's independence reflects the intensity of the forces ranged against him rather than any personal shortcomings he might have had as a leader. Indeed the evidence suggests a man of great ability who worked skilfully in very different social and political environments. This was shown within the Zulu kingdom, in the first forty years of Cetshwayo's life during his rise to power, when he played an important part in the preservation of Zulu independence at a time when many African communities were being undermined by the forces of colonialism. However Cetshwayo's very success marked him and his people out as the target for the most vigorous exercise of force the British used against any African society in southern Africa.

Cetshwayo's talents in diplomacy were well demonstrated after the war when he successfully persuaded the British government to return him to Zululand. Although his appeals for British support were expressed in terms of loyalty to 'England' and 'the Queen', they were in fact based on a sound assessment of British interests and strategy in southern Africa at the time; Cetshwayo was returned because it was thought he could serve British interests best by establishing a strong African government in a strategically significant area. However this plan conflicted with the objectives of certain influential officials in the colony of Natal and they succeeded in reducing Cetshwayo's power and authority in Zululand. Thus Cetshwayo returned without the material and political strength which had been the prime factor in Britain's initial calculation, and consequently he was left only with moral arguments to persuade Britian to continue supporting him. As a result Britain stood aside and let the civil war take its course, and when the king was dead, and the material strength of the nation was gone, distributed the spoils between herself and those forces which for so long had sought to overthrow the power of the Zulu king.

NOTES

[1] G. W. Cox, *The Life of John William Colenso, D. D., Bishop of Natal* (London, 1888), Vol. II, p. 451.

[2] Colonial Office: 179/162, minute by E. Fairfield, 25 April 1885.

[3] *British Parliamentary Papers (B.P.P.)*: C.2079, no. 39: Shepstone to Carnarvon, 2 January 1878.

[4] 'Extracts from the Blue Books' (privately printed, Bishopstowe), p. 263.

[5] *Ibid.*, p. 282.

[6] C. Vijn, *Cetshwayo's Dutchman . . .* (London, 1880), pp. 38–9.

[7] Cox, *Life of Colenso*, Vol. II, pp. 538–9. Sobantu (Father of the People) was Colenso's Zulu name.

[8] *B.P.P.*: C.3247, no. 3, encl. 2: Cetshwayo to Kimberley, 15 July 1881.

[9] W. Campbell, *With Cetshwayo in the Inkandhla and the present state of the Zulu question* (Durban, 1883), p. 11.

[10] Quoted J. W. Colenso, 'Digest on Zulu affairs (privately printed, Bishopstowe), p. 570.

[11] *Ibid.*, p. 23.

[12] R. C. A. Samuelson, *Long, Long Ago* (Durban, 1929), p. 244.

FURTHER READING

S. Marks, *Reluctant Rebellion* (Oxford, 1970).

D. R. Morris, *The Washing of the Spears* (New York, 1965).

E. Brookes and C. de B. Webb, *A History of Natal* (Pietermaritzburg, 1965).

C. de B. Webb, 'Great Britain and the Zulu People', in L. Thompson, ed., *African Societies in Southern Africa* (London, 1969).

F. E. Colenso, *The Ruin of Zululand* (London, 1884–5), 2 vols.

J. J. Guy, 'The Destruction of the Zulu Kingdom: the Civil War in Zululand, 1879–1884', Ph.D. thesis, University of London, 1975.

6
Masopha
c.1820—99

Moshoeshoe, creator of the Sotho nation, resisted and
collaborated with the white man in almost equal measure.
Masopha, the third son in his first house, became the
arch resister among the southern Sotho. Having fought
against both African and Afrikaner enemies during his
father's lifetime, he then opposed the Cape administration in Basutoland in the 1870s. His resistance during
the 'Gun War' was largely instrumental in deciding the
Cape to hand the territory back to the British. Under
British rule he continued to struggle to retain his
independence and feuded with the Sotho Paramount until
defeated in battle in 1898.

When the Kingdom of Lesotho was given its independence by
Britain in 1966, it commemorated Moshoeshoe,[1] its founder, as
the originator of its nationhood. Yet, another chief had a claim to
be remembered as well—Masopha, third son of Moshoeshoe by
his first wife, 'MaMohato. Had he not led his country in the only
successful revolt of an African people under Cape rule, it is
almost certain that today Lesotho would be part of the Republic
of South Africa.

Masopha was born in about 1820 and was the son who most
closely resembled his father. At an early age he came under the
influence of the French Evangelical Society missionaries (who
had been welcomed by Moshoeshoe in 1833 as missionaries to
the Sotho), and was educated by them. In 1841 he was baptized
into the church under the name of David. Highly intelligent, he
was in 1845 the senior of three of Moshoeshoe's sons who
accompanied one of the missionaries on a visit to Cape Town,
where they stayed for a year, learning English and the ways of
the white man. Although Masopha did not keep up his reading
and writing, his experience in the Colony was to stand him in
good stead in later years. By temperament he was a generous

11 Masopha

man and was deeply attached to Casalis, the leading missionary, but in 1845 he left the church, angered by missionary opposition to a war against a neighbouring chief which he and many other Sotho were convinced was just. He subsequently became for the rest of his life, to the missionaries' distress, an ardent supporter of many Sotho customs opposed by the church.

He enjoyed a good relationship with his father, to whom he was fiercely loyal, and with some of his half brothers acted as a messenger for Moshoeshoe. Glimpses of him come through the many reports of him in this role, dealing with the Afrikaners and British during the years before Lesotho became a British colony. One account by a British army official, for example, tells of a visit Masopha and a junior brother paid to a British camp with a message from their father in 1852:

> [They] walked round the camp with the Assistant-Commissioner, took great interest in everything, and in their remarks and questions showed a degree of information and intelligence that perfectly astonished us. . . . Both spoke English most fluently and correctly, having been educated at Cape Town, and talked of our Peninsular War, of which they had read in Napier's History! They went into many of the officers' tents; closely examined all the rifles and pistols they saw, and were especially taken with some large conical and Minié bullets, talking earnestly about them with each other in their language. Promising to return next day with their father, they took their leave in the evening with great politeness.[2]

By the early 1850s Masopha was winning a name for himself as the most daring of Moshoeshoe's sons, taking part in 1852 in a raid against the neighbouring Newlanders and Rolong living in the vicinity of Bloemfontein, and displaying great bravery both in the battle of the Berea, when the British invaded Lesotho, and in the 1853 Sotho campaign in which Moshoeshoe's old enemy, Sekonyela, was finally defeated. Soon afterwards, in 1854, Moshoeshoe sent Masopha to establish a village in the central area of Lesotho, where he soon built up a considerable following. With his full brothers, he became one of Moshoeshoe's most powerful subordinates and remained an adviser to his father.

In 1858 the Orange Free State attacked Lesotho, after increasingly bitter disputes between the two sides over stock theft and land encroachment. Masopha participated both in the war—which ended with the Sotho undefeated—and in the peace negotiations which followed. He fought again in the hostilities which broke out between the Sotho and Free State in 1865, and was routed with heavy losses when he tried to defend his village on the Berea plateau. He then withdrew to his father's stronghold of Thaba Bosiu, where he enhanced his reputation for courage and acted as Moshoeshoe's leading military adviser. The

12 Moshoeshoe in 1860

Sotho, however, lost the war, and in the peace treaty were deprived of so much of the land essential for their survival that further hostilities were inevitable. These broke out again in 1867. By the following year the Sotho were on the verge of defeat by the Free State when, as a result of Moshoeshoe's frequent and increasingly urgent requests, the British government finally agreed to bring Lesotho under British rule and protection. The country was annexed under the name of 'Basutoland'. Further hostilities and delays were to follow (Moshoeshoe died in 1870 just before the last formalities were completed), but by 1871 both the Sotho and the Orange Free State had accepted the division of land laid down in the peace treaty, and the British administration at last began to establish itself in the much diminished territory that now formed Basutoland.

The Advent of Cape Rule

As a first step, the country was divided into districts, which immediately brought the administration into confrontation with Masopha. The chief was by then in his early fifties and had a great deal of influence with the Sotho, both because of his bravery in the war against the Free State and from acting as his father's righthand man in the old chief's declining years. On Moshoeshoe's death, Letsie, his heir, had stayed at his village of Matsieng, and it was Masopha who had moved to Thaba Bosiu, the original citadel of the Sotho nation. As the mountain was already established as the customary home of the Paramount, on the division of Basutoland into districts, Masopha was allocated the Berea District and ordered by the High Commissioner's Agent to move from Thaba Bosiu. He did not move, however, and there followed a tussle of wills between him and the administration, which lasted until the middle of 1874. The High Commissioner felt that:

> [Masopha's] bravery during the late war, and his great influence over the 'Tribe', render it all the less desirable that he should be allowed to enjoy the prestige of residing at a stronghold—for which especially since it became the burial place of 'Moshesh', the Basutos entertain a superstitious reverence which might easily be turned to account by an ambitious man desirous of subverting the authority, or disturbing the peace of the country of his more peacefully disposed elder brothers.[3]

And once having taken a stand on the matter, the local administration, while not agreeing, felt that its loss of face would be too great if it gave way. Eventually Masopha agreed to move, whereupon the administration, with honour satisfied and fearing a change of mind, hastily called a meeting of Letsie, Masopha, and their people and announced that the boundary had been redrawn to include Masopha's present village within the adjacent Berea District, as an act of clemency by the government.

It is questionable how far Masopha had ulterior motives in insisting on remaining near Thaba Bosiu, but the five-year struggle built up a reservoir of bad feeling between him and the government, and he became the obvious champion to whom tribesmen could look whenever anti-government agitation arose, a situation little altered by his subsequent behaviour. Britain had late in 1871 transferred Basutoland to the Cape Colony, to be ruled directly from Cape Town, and the Cape administration was deliberately implementing a policy of undermining the chiefs and replacing their courts with those of the magistrates. Not surprisingly, the chiefs objected, and due to local political developments, of the three major chiefs in the country, Masopha was in the best position to oppose the administration. Letsie, the timid Paramount, was too afraid of challenges from his brothers to alienate the administration which supported him; and Molapo, the second brother, alienated both his powerful neighbours, the Zulu, and some sections of the Sotho when in 1873 he helped the administration capture Langalibalele, a rebel chief who fled to him for protection from Natal. Molapo too, therefore, felt the need for protection and support from the administration. But Masopha was under no such constraints. The 1874 report of the magistrate stationed with him noted that: 'the Chief Masupha,[4] while professing loyalty before any one favourable towards the Government, does, I regret to say, all he dares to keep his followers from becoming acquainted with, and obeying the instructions and laws of the Government, and to uphold the continuance of their heathenish customs.'[5] In the ensuing five years, Masopha not only continued this behaviour, but also clashed openly with his magistrate despite strenuous efforts by the administration to avoid confrontation; and at the annual national meetings of the Sotho (which were attended by the magistrates and missionaries) it was he who spoke out against the policy of depriving the chiefs of their judicial powers.

Whether he could ever have mustered sufficient support to oppose the administration successfully, had the Cape government not made a major policy blunder, is extremely doubtful. In 1878 it decided, as part of a wider policy in the African territories which it ruled, that the Sotho should be disarmed. This policy was announced to them by the Cape Prime Minister at the annual national meeting in October 1879. To the Sotho, such an idea was anathema. Over at least the preceding six years there had been a great increase in gun buying. These guns were often purchased out of wages earned at the diamond fields, and each gun represented hours of labour for the buyer. Guns might also become necessary to defend their land once more were the white man ever to abandon Basutoland again (the British had taken it over in 1848 and abandoned it six years later). Most important, guns were considered a sign of manhood: to be disarmed was regarded by the Sotho as equivalent to being reduced to the status of children. Finally, the Sotho interpreted the disarmament policy as a sign that the administration distrusted them. No argument advanced by the government or missionaries could overcome the combined force of these considerations. If any issue could unite the whole nation behind any available Sotho leader, this was it.

The most obvious leader was not available. The Paramount Chief Letsie was old, obese, sick and vacillating, much under the influence of the Governor's Agent and the missionaries, and unwilling to lead a revolt which, if successful, could have disastrous results for Basutoland, and possibly his own Paramountcy. He therefore set out to do all in his power to avert the armed resistance which he foresaw would follow if the government tried forcibly to disarm the Sotho. However, petitions to the Governor and the Queen failed, and even a Sotho delegation sent to petition the Cape parliament was unable to get the policy altered. Despite all this, Letsie advised submission rather than violence, but was in the uncomfortable position of advocating a policy to which the vast majority of his people and fellow chiefs were opposed, and from which there now seemed no escape short of armed revolt. Masopha's position was daily strengthening as leader of the majority view, and prophetesses among the Sotho began to hail him as the next Paramount. To Lerotholi, Letsie's heir, it became obvious that if he were to retain the Paramountcy, he would have to join his powerful uncle in opposition to disarmament.

The magistrates attempted to persuade the people to surrender their weapons voluntarily, but those that did so were promptly attacked by the rebel chiefs, had all their goods confiscated, and were sometimes killed fighting to protect them. The magistrates were powerless to assist. For enforcing government orders, they had always relied on the co-operation of the chiefs and people, or at least on them not defying magisterial orders. Now both respect and obedience rapidly disappeared and the country soon degenerated into anarchy. Masopha fortified Thaba Bosiu, and after several 'loyal' villages were attacked in his district, his magistrate was ordered to fall back on Maseru, the capital, with his clerk and police, since they could not hope to withstand a similar attack from Masopha. But open warfare still did not break out: Masopha refused to allow his warriors to attack Maseru, and the magistracy at Berea remained untouched. Letsie, taking heart, led a thousand men to Thaba Bosiu, where he met Masopha and Lerotholi, who were waiting there with seven or eight hundred fully armed men; but nine days of tense negotiation ended in deadlock. The Prime Minister of the Cape then came to Basutoland in a last-minute attempt to prevent full-scale rebellion, and met the Sotho at a national meeting where he offered new disarmament terms. Lerotholi, however, refused to surrender any guns, and Masopha did not even attend the meeting. Instead, he simultaneously held a gathering at which his young warriors were prepared for war. With all hope of compromise gone, the inevitable outbreak came a few days later in September 1880: troops were moved into Basutoland to garrison the magistracies, and were attacked by Lerotholi shortly after they crossed the border. The Gun War had finally broken out.

The Gun War and After

The war lasted for seven months, with Masopha blockading Maseru and a number of other magistracies being besieged. One magistrate was killed and Lerotholi led a series of lightning attacks on the Cape forces, who were unable to pin him down. The far from negligible minority of the nation which had remained loyal to the government was forced to take refuge in camps huddled round the magistracies, and their rations proved an added drain on Cape resources. By the time that the Cape expenses for the war had reached £3,000,000, the Cape government was exceedingly anxious to make peace. It entered into negotiations with Lerotholi and eventually, with the Cape Governor acting as arbitrator, the Sotho accepted the terms of his Award and the Gun War ended.

On the immediate issue of disarmament, Masopha and Lerotholi had won. The Award nominally provided for disarmament, but the licensing of guns would be freely allowed, and compensation would be paid for those surrendered. As it was clear that the Cape could no longer enforce the disarmament provision, or anything else, the question of disarmament became purely theoretical. At this point Lerotholi's and Masopha's interests, never identical, diverged radically. Given the stresses inherent in Sotho chiefdoms, Masopha had always been a potential challenger to

Letsie's—and hence Lerotholi's—Paramountcy. Lerotholi was particularly vulnerable, for, as son of Letsie's second rather than first wife, his claim to succeed Letsie was open to question according to Sotho law. While the majority of the people favoured the government, as they did in the first eight or nine years of Cape rule, it was obviously in Lerotholi's interest to be loyal to the government and secure its backing against his uncle. But when the disarmament issue swung the people against the government, and its lack of power became increasingly evident, Lerotholi ran every risk of being supplanted by Masopha unless he joined him in his popular cause. This he did, and there is evidence that even Letsie kept his options open by remaining in touch with the rebels throughout the war. Now, with the question of disarmament settled and the people anxious for peace, Lerotholi was in a stronger position to revert to government support. It is known that there was no love lost between him and his uncle, and whether he and Masopha were on the same or opposing sides, Masopha remained a threat to his position. Lerotholi therefore once more reverted to the role of loyal heir to a loyal chief, and promptly found himself with a problem partly of his own making, but greatly aggravated by Masopha.

The Award had provided not only for disarmament, but also for a fine of five thousand cattle, together with compensation for traders and those who had remained loyal to the government. However, most chiefs were unwilling or unable to persuade their people to surrender the cattle required. This was serious for the administration and hence for Lerotholi. Ultimately the re-establishment of magisterial rule depended on the magistrates' ability to secure the property and safeguard the rights of anyone who entrusted himself to government justice, and this the magistrates would have had difficulty in doing even had there been no opposition party in the country. Unfortunately there was: Masopha at first refused to accept the Governor's Award at all. He was only coerced into nominally doing so in September 1881, when Sauer, the Cape Secretary for Native Affairs, arrived in Basutoland and began to organize an expedition by Letsie and Lerotholi against him. However, as soon as Sauer returned to Cape Town, having already withdrawn all colonial troops except the Cape Carbineers, the problem reappeared: Masopha, from his mountain-top, announced his refusal to submit. An attempt by the Governor's Agent, with Letsie and Lerotholi's warriors, to capture him on 24 January failed. A large part of Basutoland remained in a state of anarchy similar to that which had prevailed before the war: Masopha and his allies were back in the saddle and intended to stay there.

In the period between 1882 and late 1883 the Cape government tried a number of policies to regain control. All were equally ineffective, and as the government became increasingly desperate, the solutions tried became more and more unpredictable. One even involved sending Major-General Charles Gordon ('Chinese Gordon', later to be killed in Khartoum) to visit Masopha in the hope that he would live up to his reputation for being able to 'manage native people' and, by his intense, mesmeric personality, bring Masopha to heel. However, his visit coincided with an expedition against Masopha by Letsie and Lerotholi, also sanctioned by the government in a remarkably muddle-headed clash of policies. This forced Gordon to leave Thaba Bosiu in the middle of his negotiations, and obliged Lerotholi to delay his attack so long that most of his men left for home before the attack on Thaba Bosiu could take place. The government was left not only looking even more ridiculous than before, but suspected of treachery by Lerotholi. In desperation, the Secretary of Native Affairs visited Basutoland again in October 1882 and had a meeting with Masopha and about a thousand of his people at Thaba Bosiu. Masopha was adamant that they did not wish to have a magistrate or pay taxes. Faced with this situation, the Cape government in January 1883 put forward a policy for internal indirect rule through the chiefs. It was a complete reversal of normal Cape policy on ruling African areas and an indication of how much at a loss the Cape was on what to do about Basutoland. However, when it was placed before the nation at a meeting in April, the consent of those who attended, including Letsie, was half-hearted, and Masopha and his supporters refused to attend at all. Though the policy might have been acceptable even to Masopha in other circumstances, the Cape government was by then completely discredited.

The government, faced with a situation with which it felt unable to cope, opened negotiations with the British government at the beginning of May to hand over the country to its care. On 29 November a national meeting was called to ask the nation whether it was willing to be ruled by Britain or would prefer abandonment. With the land-hungry Orange Free State on their borders, the former seemed the lesser of two evils to most Sotho. Some three thousand assembled, together with the Paramount and most of the leading chiefs, but of the three leading chiefs conspicuously absent, Masopha was the senior. Those chiefs and headmen present signed a document expressing their willingness to come under British rule again. They represented over 110,000 people; the absent chiefs represented about 20,000. Masopha, to emphasize his rejection of the proposals, held a meeting of his own at which he demanded complete self-government, but the British government decided in mid-December that the Sotho majority was large enough to warrant it accepting Basutoland. The transfer took place on 18 March 1884, and the new code of regulations promulgated by the High Commissioner gave the chiefs far greater freedom from magisterial control than had been allowed under Cape rule.

Masopha had achieved his original aim of regaining control over his people and the right to exercise his judicial and most other forms of chiefly authority. Why then did he reject British rule? The Bloemfontein newspaper, *The Friend of the Free State*, speculated that his defiance might be part of a national plot 'in order that the Basutos, when the time comes for them to kick up their heels again, may say, "We never agreed as a united people to the Imperial Government resuming rule over us".'[6] If this were so, the lack of interference by the British Resident Commissioner made it unnecessary ever to resort to the plan. Or did Masopha fear encroachment on the chiefs' powers by British officials once they were installed? Or did his resistance indicate, as some suspected, that by the time the Cape government left Basutoland he was set on gaining full independence from Letsie, if not the Paramount Chieftanship for himself? He must have realized that while the British remained able to control the country through the legitimate Paramount and his heir, neither independence nor a seizure of power would be possible.

If independence was his aim, he never achieved it. He continued to forment trouble between his nephews who lived near him, in each case assisting one side in order to obtain their support. These quarrels frequently led to fighting, the victors invariably confiscating as much of the property of those defeated as they could find. The British magistrates were not strong enough to intervene in such skirmishes, or even to punish Masopha when he had three men put to death for witchcraft. Eventually, however, he and Lesaoana, his cousin, had a serious fight in which about fifty men were killed. Each chief, anxious for government support, appealed for arbitration, and their acceptance of the resulting decision on their dispute greatly strengthened the government's position in the eyes of the Sotho. Masopha, finding himself increasingly isolated and out of touch with the nation, asked the Resident Commissioner in February 1886 to place a magistrate in his district. The man who was sent for the first four months, Godfrey Lagden, was able to collect taxes and, for the first time in six years, re-establish a magistracy in the district. In later years, even after he had become Resident Commissioner and clashed repeatedly with Masopha, Lagden recorded that he always admired Masopha's 'attractive personality and manliness'.

Masopha under British Rule

With the return of Masopha and his supporters to the government fold, the country was for the first time united, and when the Resident Commissioner held the country's first regular annual national meeting since the British administration had taken over, Masopha and every other leading chief were among those who attended. However, although Masopha was in his late sixties, he showed little sign of mellowing. When in 1887 he and Lesaoana again fell out over a land dispute, the resulting fight led to over twenty men being killed and many wounded. Letsie, incensed, sent an expedition against Masopha, who appealed for protection to the Resident Commissioner and paid the government fine of a thousand head of cattle. But although he might have become reconciled to submission to Letsie, submission to Lerotholi was a different matter. When Letsie died in November 1891, he supported a younger son of Letsie in challenging Lerotholi as the new Paramount. The young rebel was brought to heel and heavily fined, but not before the country had reached the brink of civil war. Thereafter no further disturbances emanated from Masopha for several years, until in 1897 a conflict over land with one of the sons of a deceased brother led to fighting in which several men were killed. Lagden, who was by then Resident Commissioner, has described how he summoned Masopha to appear before a National Council to deal with the case. Masopha 'first refused to go and then attended with a large body of men whose arms were concealed beneath their blankets. Though sullenly submitting to a judgment imposing fines on those immediately responsible for the disturbance, he indulged in angry recriminations with the Paramount Chief during the sitting of the Court, which broke up in confusion.'[7] The Paramount had to reoccupy the land forcibly with 1,500 men to uphold the decision of the court, which further aggravated the situation.

The feud between Masopha and Lerotholi came to a head a few months later. In November 1897 a junior son of Masopha raided the Orange Free State and seized a woman who had run away from her husband in Lesotho. He was arrested in the Free State and sentenced to imprisonment with lashes, but managed to break jail and rejoin his father. Masopha, when ordered to surrender him to justice, not only refused to do so, but declared he would resist any attempt at arrest. Lagden called upon Lerotholi to enforce the law and effect the arrest, but only when all attempts at persuasion had failed did the Paramount march on Masopha with every man be could muster. Masopha, true to the last to his Sotho name of 'the Wildebeest', decided to fight. He evacuated Thaba Bosiu to take up a strong position on the plateau overlooking the Phutiatsana, and the two armies, each of some ten thousand men, faced each other across the river. The question was no longer merely the surrender of a criminal: it was a battle for supremacy between rival sections of the tribe.

On 5 January 1898 Lerotholi attacked and the stronghold fell next day. The losses were small, but not the penalties which followed. Masopha formally surrendered his son, who was tried and sentenced to prison. Masopha himself was heavily fined, deprived of his district chieftainship, and forbidden to reoccupy his village at Thaba Bosiu, the historic fortifications of which were dismantled. The following year he died, aged seventy-eight, a broken old man.

And yet, although he never became Paramount, he had, despite himself, set his country on the road to the independence which he sought. Had he not determinedly headed opposition to magisterial rule, through all attempts after the Gun War to reimpose it, the Cape would have remained in Basutoland, which would have suffered the fate of the other Cape-ruled African areas that eventually came under the laws of the Union of South Africa. Masopha's continued opposition sapped the Cape government's confidence in its ability to rule Basutoland, and led eventually to its handing the country back to an imperial power which in time gave its African territories independence. Masopha could not have foreseen the eventual result of his resistance to Cape rule; and had he won his final battle, his victory would probably have spelt disaster for his country. The British would almost certainly have felt obliged to abandon Basutoland to the mercy of its neighbours, since the defeat for the Paramount's forces would have left them with no means of enforcing their decisions unless they had imported expensive imperial troops. Had Basutoland been abandoned, its own past history and that of other chiefdoms in similar positions indicate that it would very probably have been absorbed piecemeal into the Orange Free State, leaving the Sotho living as squatters on white-owned farms. Ironically, Masopha's final defeat ensured that his people survived as an independent nation, but equally, without his victory against the Cape it is very unlikely that today his country would be recognized as the independent Kingdom of Lesotho.

NOTES

[1] The Sotho language has two systems of orthography, one of which is used in Lesotho and the other in the Republic of South Africa. The former has been adopted here.

[2] W. R. King, *Campaigning in Kaffirland* (London, 2nd edn., 1855), pp. 310–11.

[3] Cape Archives, Native Affairs Department 272: High Commissioner to High Commissioner's Agent, 2 September 1871, enclosed in Governor's Agent to Secretary for Native Affairs, no. 12, 21 November 1873.

[4] Many words are spelt in a variety of ways in the documents of this period, since Sotho orthography was not yet settled. 'Masopha' is also spelt 'Masupha' and 'Masupa'.

[5] *Cape Parliamentary Papers*, G. 21–75, p. 9.

[6] *The Friend of the Free State*, 6 December 1883.

[7] G. Lagden, *The Basutos* (London, 1909), Vol. II, pp. 593–4.

FURTHER READING

E. Bradlow, 'The Cape Government's rule of Basutoland 1871–1883', *Archives Year Book for South African History*, 1968, Part II.

E. Casalis, *The Basutos* (London, 1861).

R. C. Germond, *Chronicles of Basutoland* (Morija, 1967).

G. Lagden, *The Basutos* (London, 1909), 2 vols.

E. S. Smith, *The Mabilles of Basutoland* (London, 1939).

G. Tylden, *The Rise of the Basuto* (Cape Town, 1950).

J. Widdicombe, *Fourteen Years in Basutoland* (London, 1891).

7
Adam Kok III
1811–75

Great-grandson of Adam Kok I, Adam Kok III ruled the eastern Griqua at Philippolis from 1837 until the early 1860s, when he and his people trekked across the Drakensberg to found a new state in what became known as Griqualand East. After more than a decade of independence there, the Griquas suddenly found themselves taken under British control in 1874. Kok retained a measure of power, but died at the end of the following year.

The place of Adam Kok within nineteenth-century South African history derives essentially from the ambiguity of the Griquas within the Southern African social order. On the one hand they were dark-skinned, being the descendants of every conceivable racial group of South Africa. Among their ancestors were large numbers of Khoisan, so that the remnants of Khoi tribal organization may be rather dimly perceived in the patriarchal style of government of the first Griqua leaders, in particular Adam Kok's grandfather, Cornelis Kok I. On a linguistic level, this inheritance also remained of importance, Adam's wife, for instance, was not fluent in any other tongue except for the now extinct Cape Khoi. However, this language was slowly ousted by Dutch, clearly in one of its more creolized forms. This linguistic shift symbolizes the major tension within Griqua history, which Adam Kok recognized but could not resolve, because the solution was well outside the power of the Griquas.

But for the colour of their skins, the Griquas had all the aspirations, and many of the attributes, of the white ruling class which was slowly taking over control of South Africa. The Griquas were landowners, and, when they had the opportunity, orientated towards markets. They were receptive towards new economic opportunities. In the 1830s the Boers of the north-east Cape com-

13 Adam Kok III

plained that the access that the Griquas denied them to the rich pastures north of the Orange—at least temporarily—gave the Griquas an unfair advantage in the cattle markets of Graaff-Reinet and Grahamstown, while two decades later the Griquas took to the keeping of merino sheep at least as quickly as did their Boer neighbours. They were also Christian, both in terms of the image they wished to project—the first code of laws the Griquas issued included an outlawing of polygamy—and in fact, although they naturally did not all satisfy the rigorous standards of the missionaries in this regard. They were, many of them, literate. Adam Kok himself had a large, legible, if somewhat unformed and schoolboyish hand. They were often employers of Africans as labourers, and sometimes reached the apogee of civilization by living as rentiers on the proceeds of African peasant farming. In short, they behaved in much the same ways as the Europeans of southern Africa. But their skin colour was 'wrong'. Therefore, throughout the century, pressure was exerted on them by those who considered putative skin-colour to be of importance for acceptance into the ruling class of South African society, to force the Griquas from their position of power. In this, probably unconscious process, the white ruling class succeeded. Except where they have 'passed' for white, the descendants of the Griquas are no longer landowners, nor particularly prosperous. But it was in the attempt to defend the Griquas from the erosion of their rights and position that Adam Kok spent the major part of his life.

Before they could lose their heritage, however, the Griquas had to acquire it. Adam Kok was instrumental in helping the Griquas in the later stages of their search for wealth and respectability. He was born near what is now Griquatown in the northern Cape, on 11 December 1811.[1] This was about the time that his father, also called Adam, was taking over from Cornelis as head of the large Kok clan, which was the richest and most important in the half-caste Khoi society which had established itself along the Orange river valley. This society was, in many ways, the cutting edge of colonial society emanating ultimately from Cape Town. It formed the link between the Cape colony and the Tswana, trading cattle south and cloth and iron northwards, while it was itself a producer of cattle and of various grains. However, in the decade from 1816 to 1826, it was rent by a long series of civil wars, and eventually a large number of Griquas under the leadership of the elder Adam moved from the northern Cape east to what is now the southern Orange Free State, where they centred their community on the London Mission Society station of Philippolis.

Philippolis

The area around Philippolis over which the Griquas slowly spread was good cattle and sheep country, although in the course of the nineteenth century the veld slowly deteriorated as karroo bushes spread north at the expense of the highland sweet grass-veld. Rains were too uncertain to make agriculture a viable proposition, especially as there was not enough permanent water to allow irrigation, but this did not greatly trouble the Griquas who, like their Boer reference group, were accustomed to an essentially pastoral economy. But such an economy, when connected with rapid population growth of both humans and stock, demands a continually expanding land area in order to be viable. Thus the Griquas found themselves in the main path of expansion of the trekboers of the north-eastern Cape, who were being forced by a series of droughts to spill north of the Orange in the movement that culminated in the Great Trek. From the beginning of the 1830s onwards, there were always Boers residing, more or less permanently, in the area which the Philippolis Captaincy claimed as its territory.

Politically, although the Kok family remained in nominal control of Philippolis, the leading figure in the Captaincy was the Government Secretary, Hendrick Hendricks. He was Adam Kok III's brother-in-law, but he owed the maintainance of his position not so much to nepotism as to the sharpness of his political intelligence. Especially while the elder Adam, who could not read, was alive, Hendricks held the conduct of the relationships of the Griquas with other peoples mainly in his own hands. He also played a leading role in the labyrinthine internal Philippolis politics, especially as they developed around the problem of succession to the elder and ailing Adam. Until 1829 everything was clear. Dam, as he was known, was planning to retire in favour of his eldest son, Cornelis. But in that year Cornelis died. The Griquas were then left with a choice between his two remaining legitimate sons, Abraham and Adam. The two brothers represented very different tendencies within the Griqua state. Abraham the elder son who was illiterate, and still lived in a Khoisan mat hut, seems to have seen the Griqua future

14 Philippolis

as essentially predatory, either ruling Africans or, preferably, stealing their cattle. In particular, the vast Ndebele herds exercised a fascination for him, as they had for many Griquas over the previous decade. Many others, however, saw that such a mode of existence was no longer viable in the long term, as the expansion of Boer settlement and, in its wake, British colonial authority could only lead to a general pacification of the interior of southern Africa, or at least to an ordering of conflict which would place those who behaved as Abraham beyond the pale of the society to which the Griquas (many of whose ancestors, it must be remembered, had been outcasts from the colony) aspired. It was this latter party that Adam headed.

Nevertheless, in the leadership election, held on 26 January 1836, four months after old Dam's death, Abraham won by 168 votes to 68. He seems to have done so because he received the support of those who valued his legitimacy as the elder brother and, at the same time, considered that he was sufficiently weak in character to be effectively controlled. Moreover, the mission party was temporarily in bad odour and much of this rubbed off on Adam, their evident representative. However Abraham was an unmitigated disaster. His attempt to raid the Ndebele failed badly and he was deserted by most of his followers, including, most significantly, Hendricks. By the middle of 1837, he was ousted, and, after being repulsed in his attempt to regain power by coup de main, he disappeared from the scene. He must have died shortly afterwards because, in what must have been an attempt to reconcile some of Abraham's supporters, Adam shortly afterwards married the woman who had been Abraham's wife and who belonged to the influential Pienaar family. This clearly consolidated his position and he reigned unchallenged for the subsequent thirty-eight years of his life. The marriage did not prove fruitful, however, and Adam left no descendants.

When he assumed power, Adam was still a young man, aged twenty-five. He had already had a certain amount of experience as an assistant to his father and in arranging a treaty with Andries Waterboer, the head of the other Griqua state, centred on Griquatown, but in the first years of his reign he did not dominate the political life of Philippolis. Only slowly did he assert his position against that of Hendrick Hendricks, who remained Government secretary until 1850. Nevertheless, Adam seems slowly to have begun to take decisions himself, and came to be seen as more than a figurehead, even if he left much of the oratory to the eloquent Hendricks. It was a time when the Griquas needed strong leadership, and in general they seem to have got it.

Throughout the 1840s, the Captaincy was at the heart of the conflict between the Voortrekkers and the British government as to the exercise of authority on the High Veld. Following the British annexation of Natal, the more militant Afrikaners had returned across the Drakensberg and laid claim to all the territory north of the Orange river, which formed the northern boundary of the Cape Colony. This claim would therefore have included the Philippolis Captaincy, although at times such Boer leaders as Potgieter disclaimed any intention of ruling anyone except the Voortrekker community. Nevertheless, the Griquas saw their own independence threatened by the establishment of Boer power—correctly as events turned out—and attempted to preserve it by reliance on the British. This was in effect their only alternative, even if it was to prove no more valuable or lasting. It was thus very largely the Griquas who were responsible for bringing the British troops north of the Orange to contest Boer control of southern Transorangia. Thus in 1842, it was Kok who informed the British authorities of the Boers' intention to raise a standard at Alleman's drift on the Orange, proclaiming their sovereignty over the land to the north, an action, which, after a certain amount of to-ing and fro-ing, led eventually to the bloodless dispersal of the Boer laager by the redcoats under Lieutenant-Colonel Hare. Two years later, Kok again almost provoked war by arresting a Boer named van Staden and sending him to Colesberg, in the Cape Colony, to stand trial for murdering an Englishman, and by imposing regulations on the amount of brandy that Boers could carry north of the Orange. This did not lead to a major confrontation only because the Boers were then occupied in reorganizing their own society, setting up Potgieter as the head of a theoretically united *maatschappy* stretching from the Orange to the Limpopo. A year later, when Kok attempted to arrest another Boer, this time for the more minor offence of kidnapping two Tswana subjects of the Griquas, conflict did break out. For about two weeks, the Boers and the Griquas fired shots at each other, at the extreme range of their rather inaccurate weapons. Casualties were minimal, but the Griquas lost a large number of their cattle, which they did not recover even after the British troops had once again come north and dispersed the Boers in a single charge at the battle of Zwartkoppies.

Clearly, the political structure of the interior of southern Africa was far from stable at this time. After two bouts of treaty-making had failed, the British government decided to annex the area between the Vaal and the Orange early in 1848 in an attempt to establish a more lasting order and to develop an alliance with the most likely class of collaborators in the area, the Boers. At least, this is to be charitable to them and to ascribe coherent geopolitical motives to the eccentric governor, Sir Harry Smith, who saw the solution to all problems in the strength of his own personality and the imposition of his own prestige. In his efforts to set up the Orange River Sovereignty, he was forced to compel the Griquas to agree to the abrogation of the treaties they had made with the British government over the last decade. This at least gave them some protection against the alienation of their land to the Boers who were settling on it and paying a nominal rent to the poorest members of the Philippolis community. Smith was able to do this by the simple, if brutal, expedient of threatening to hang Adam Kok. In this way, despite their protests, the Griquas became for a time British subjects, but the Orange River Sovereignty solved no problems and only involved the British in paying for, and losing wars against the Sotho. After six years, therefore, they managed to extricate themselves from the obligations they had taken on and arranged for the founding, first of the South African Republic in the Transvaal and then for that of the Orange Free State, whose official area of jurisdiction included the whole area of the Captaincy of Philippolis.

Throughout these twists and turns of British policy, the Griquas remained loyal to the belief that, in the end, the British would not let them down and their best interests would be served by persuading the British to impose a state of equal competition between Griqua, Boer and Briton. In this they were sorely mistaken, but it remains a puzzle why their policy seems to have been so uniformly short-sighted. Hendricks, right at the end of his career, may have attempted to forge an alliance with the Boers on the basis of their common position as land-owners and employers of labour, but even here the evidence is uncertain. No such initiatives, however, came from Adam Kok. In large part, this derived from the desire of the Griquas to be accepted as civilized members of the southern African community, which they associated largely with the British.

However, there was a deeper level of confusion in their attitude—to ally with the Boers and the British on the basis of their common landowning would have forced the richer Griquas to slough off their poorer fellows. This they were never prepared to do. Adam Kok clearly saw himself as the leader of his people, not as the leader of the richest section of them, even during the 1850s when the wealth of many individual Griquas, including Kok and his immediate family, was increasing fast as a result of merino sheep and the widening commercial opportunities presented by the northward spread of the Cape trading network. It remains an open question how far their fellow landowners would have accepted the Griquas as equals if they had cut themselves free from their community. Probably, by the middle of the century, no such accommodation was possible, as the structure of southern African society was already based on racial ascription, which the Griquas tacitly accepted. Kok wished to remain as leader of a Griqua community on a par with the most powerful in southern Africa, rather than to enter that ruling class as a wealthy Christian in his own right. He was too much the leader of his people, and in a real sense their representative, to do otherwise.

Griqualand East

The fact that the community, by choice and circumstance, had to hold together can be seen from the decision to uproot the whole community and trek across the southern Drakensberg to what is now Griqualand East. They went because their authority over their land was being eroded by the Orange Free State government and because there was an area of apparently fertile, relatively empty land on which they could hope to re-establish their pattern of living.

Initially, Adam Kok had to conduct a certain amount of delicate negotiations with the government in Cape Town, but on the other hand he had little contact with the African chiefs of the area. He only went to visit Moshoeshoe, through whose territory the Griquas would have to trek, after the decision to leave had been made and many farms sold to the Boers. But the trek was a heroic undertaking, as the Griquas cut a wagon road across the high passes of the Drakensberg. It took them two years before they could finally debouch into the green valleys of the northern Transkei, an area which must have seemed a land of milk and honey to a people used to the aridity of the highveld, and it cost them about nine-tenths of their stock. Instead of embuing them with new energy to reconstruct their society in the new environment, the trek seems to have left the Griquas in a demoralized state from which they were only beginning to emerge when, some fifteen years later, their polity was finally annexed and extinguished by the British.

Adam Kok himself certainly shared in the general malaise. In the first years after the trek he seems to have retreated from the day-to-day running of the community, which he left more and more to his cousin, known, somewhat confusingly, as Adam 'Eta' Kok. Adam himself could not give the leadership necessary to extricate the Griquas from the collective melancholia and listlessness which travellers reported at this time. For a few years, most of the Griquas lived in the laager, a rather ramshackle, dirty collection of huts on the southern slopes of Mount Currie. Kok travelled a good deal and even had the dispiriting experience, especially for a man who had been the richest member of a prosperous community, of being distrained for debt in Port Elizabeth. At the same time, he was now well into his fifties and had lost the keen edge of his energy.

Slowly, things began to pick up. More and more Griquas began to move away from the laager and set up farms in the countryside, as they began to learn the agricultural and pastoral regime necessary in their new environment. Also, of course, this dispersal of settlement required peace with the neighbouring African tribes. As far as the Griquas were concerned, this meant that they had to dominate the Africans. A large proportion of the income of the Griqua government came from the hut-tax collected from the Hlangweni, Mfengu and Sotho of the area. From the beginning of the 1870s, they also began to extend their hegemony to the west, over Hlubi and Bhaca, especially after a short campaign in 1871 demonstrated that Griqua military might was far greater than that of their neighbours, as a result of their long familiarity with firearms. However, the African population was probably as free under Griqua rule as under any other form of alien domination; for instance, they never had to carry passes and, in some cases, assimilated to the Griquas. In large measure this was due to the personal influence of Adam Kok, who, without any children, was probably more concerned with the general, long-term good than with his own advantage. In particular, he was able to restrain the Griquas from settling on land already occupied by Africans and would punish his subjects for excessive use of force against anyone.

In his later years, Adam Kok's character comes through the sources more strongly than before, largely, it would seem, because he was more firmly in control than previously. Before the Griquas left Philippolis, travellers who visited them did not in general give a description of his character. From the late 1860s until his death in 1875, in contrast, it is much easier to gain an impression of the kindly, astute, rather melancholic old man he had become. He was always most courteous and was particularly fond of children, but he was clearly seen as a firm leader trying to help the Griquas make up for the time they had lost after the trek across the Drakensberg. This is perhaps best exemplified by the process whereby the Griquas abandoned their squalid laager and moved down the slopes of Mount Currie to found the town of Kokstad. It was clear that the site, on a bluff above the Mzimhlava river, was the right one, but it was politically difficult to make it the town because one of the leading Griquas had already claimed it and erected a mill. Kok therefore persuaded the Griquas to allow a missionary to choose a site for them, and pointed him at the land in question, so that he chose it. It was thirty years before the missionary, William Dower, discovered how he had been used.[2]

Even after the town had been laid out, it took some time before Kok could rouse the Griquas from their inertia and move down the hill to take possession of their *erven*, so that Kok could move into his new house (built, incidentally, by his erstwhile fellow Captain of Griqualand West, Nicholas Waterboer). This was situated across the main square of Kokstad from the church, and the town itself was neatly arrayed along a regular grid of narrow streets. It did not, however, have either public parks or a garden. When asked why not, Kok's reply was characteristic.

> *What, General! a Park and a Garden, like that I saw in Cape Town? General, you don't know this country, nor do you know the weaknesses of our people. Garden! Park! Oh, no; the trees would bring the birds, the birds would eat the ripe corn and we would have no bread! The shade, too, would be so nice; my people would want to sit under it all day long, instead of cultivating their farms, and by-and-by they would be beggars. No, General! we must 'wacht een beetje' for these nice things.*[3]

Clearly, it was Kok's intention to let the Griquas develop into a farming aristocracy. In their initial reconaissance of East Griqaland, they had been to Natal and had been much impressed by the plantations there. Slowly, the Griquas began to

15 Kokstad, 1878

develop the infrastructure necessary to emulate the Natalians. Land was registered, a postal service instituted and, when colonial currency was in particularly short supply, a stack of 10,000 banknotes were printed, though never issued. But this was a forlorn hope. It was not a propitious time for this sort of agricultural enterprise even for white Natalians, while the Griquas suffered the disadvantage of living much further from the ports and, paramountly, of having to face the opposition of the white colonial establishment. To have had any hope of success, the Griquas would have needed to have remained independent for a long period, but in October 1874, during an attempt to reach some sort of stabilization in the Transkei, the British government announced to the stupefied Griquas that they were taking over the government of the country. Clearly, this spelt the beginning of the economic ruin of the Griquas just as it ended their independence. The habits of a generation prevented them from resisting, at least for five years. And by this time, Kok, who could have restrained the 'rebels', was dead, run over by the wheel of his cart after a driving accident on 30 December 1875.

Kok's achievement, during his long reign, was not spectacular, nor such as to make him a heroic figure. It could not be otherwise, since, from the late 1840s when he effectively took the government of the Griqua state into his own hands he was always engaged in a holding operation. His main concerns seemed contradictory, attempting on the one hand to preserve the Griquas as a viable communal entity, and on the other to bring them to legal and economic equality with the whites who were imposing themselves as the ruling class across the whole of South Africa. This meant that the Griquas could not shed their poorest members and others judged the community by them. The measure of his success was that the Griqua state did not disintegrate earlier. His subjects also certainly thought this a great achievement: At his funeral, his cousin and colleague, Adam 'Eta', spoke as follows:

We have laid in the grave a man you all knew and loved. He is the last of his race. After him there will be no coloured king or chief in Colonial South Africa. Of Kaffir tribes, there may still be chiefs; of coloured chiefs he is the last. Take a good look into that grave. You will never look into the grave of another chief of our race. Do you realize that our nationality lies buried there? The deceased was the friend of you all. Did you ever hear of Adam Kok making an enemy? Political enemies he had, unfortunately more than his share; private enemies he had none. He had his faults—we all have; but you will bear me out, he was generous to a fault—too indulgent and gentle and yielding for a chief. There lie the remains of the one South African chief who never lifted arms nor fired a shot at a British soldier, though sometimes provoked beyond human endurance. There is not a single man here who has not received favours at his hand. If you are ever tempted to forget him, turn to the titles of your properties and see there his familiar sign manual. I have yielded to the temptation to add this much to what the minister has said because I am his near relative, and he honoured me with his confidence, and occasionally delegated to me his authority. . . . Let all questions of politics rest. Let us go home and mourn in secret and in silence, and prepare for the funeral services.[4]

NOTES

[1] The date on the memorial to Adam Kok in Kokstad.

[2] *The Kokstad Advertiser*, 19 December 1902: review of W. Dower, *The Early Annals of Kokstad and Griqualand East* (Port Elizabeth, 1902).

[3] Dower, *Early Annals*, p. 50.

[4] Dower, *Early Annals*, p. 77.

FURTHER READING

Robert Ross, *Adam Kok's Griquas; a Study in the Development of Stratification in South Africa* (Cambridge, 1976).

William Dower, *The Early Annals of Kokstad and Griqualand East* (Port Elizabeth, 1902; new edition, Pietermaritzburg, 1978).

J. S. Marais, *The Cape Coloured People* (Johannesburg, 1939), Chapter II.

M. C. Legassick, 'The Griqua, the Sotho-Tswana and the Missionaries, 1780–1840; the politics of a frontier zone', Ph.D. thesis, University of California, Los Angeles, 1969.

8
Tiyo Soga
1829−71

Ordained a minister of the United Presbyterian Church in Scotland in 1856, Tiyo Soga returned to work among his Xhosa people, first in the Ciskei and then in the Transkei. A man of two worlds, he sought to reconcile pride in his heritage with his Christian faith and western upbringing. A gifted writer, his life was cut short by his early death in 1871.

Tiyo Soga, the first ordained minister in the history of the Africans in South Africa, was the son of Old Soga, himself the son of Jotello and leading counsellor of Ngqika, head of the western Xhosa. His mother was of the amaNtinde, the daughter of Ngayi, a great wife of Soga. Tiyo was born on the Eastern Frontier of the Cape Colony in 1829, in the ancestral lands of the Ngqika section of the Xhosa, who lived between the Great Fish and Keiskamma rivers. It was a restless frontier, engulfed by periodic wars during the first half of the nineteenth century. During these wars the blacks were continually on the defensive against white colonial territorial encroachment, and this made an indelible impression on Tiyo Soga.

There were also other pressures—at an early age Tiyo Soga was exposed to Christianity. The Christian missionary advance into Xhosaland during the early nineteenth century was a formative influence on his life. His earliest education was received at Tyhume mission school, a Glasgow Missionary Society outstation, where he was taught by the Reverend William Chalmers, as well as by his own brother, Festiri.

The Sogas were an innovative family; Old Soga was the first black in Xhosaland to irrigate land for agricultural purposes and to use the plough. He also became a nominal Christian, under the influence of Ntsikana, a prophet-type religious leader. He partly renounced tribal ways and did not allow Tiyo to be cir-

cumcised, as was customary for Xhosa youths entering manhood. (Throughout his life Tiyo also opposed this practice.) From
an early age, therefore, Tiyo Soga was exposed to western
Christian civilization of the missionary variety. He found it
attractive and cultivated it.

At the age of fourteen, encouraged by Chalmers, Tiyo Soga
entered the Lovedale Seminary where the Glasgow Missionary
Society was dedicated to the education of blacks as teachers
and catechists. The seminary was multi-racial and among
the whites attending it were the sons of missionaries. However,
Tiyo Soga's education was interrupted by the 1846 Frontier
War, as the principal of Lovedale, William Govan, resigned
and took Tiyo Soga, with three other white youths, to Scotland.

The impact made by Britain upon Tiyo Soga was tremendous.
He was awe-struck by St Paul's Cathedral and terrified by hurt-
ling through railway tunnels! He soon learned that the idealized
Britain conjured up by missionaries at Lovedale was a myth,
but he survived this disillusionment and in due course grew to
love the island, its people and culture. Once in Scotland Tiyo
Soga attended school at Inchinnan and then the Glasgow Free
Church Seminary. There he was befriended by Dr William
Anderson, who baptized him in John Street Church on 7 May
1848. While in Scotland, Tiyo Soga was supported by John
Henderson, a wealthy philanthropist. But Africa called, and,
fascinated as he was by his new world, Tiyo Soga responded. On
24 October 1848 he left Glasgow for South Africa. When the
train reached Carlisle, he observed that 'We are already far from
home.' He was already clearly the victim of cultural conquest.

When Tiyo Soga reached the Cape Eastern Frontier, he helped
the Reverend John Cumming at Tyhume, and later at Igqibigha.
Then the Reverend Robert Niven hired him to teach at Uniondale,
where he lived with his sister Tause. Uniondale was the scene of
his first great trial as a black Christian. A whispering campaign
was started against him because he had not been circumcised.
Yet this local opposition to Tiyo Soga—which involved a threat
of death—was also based on a general opposition to missionaries. They were regarded as the agents of the colonial government which had steadily, during the nineteenth century,
exerted pressure on the Ngqika patrimony. There Tiyo himself
had grown up, and lived in a troubled atmosphere. Later, in the
sixties, he was able to make much of the discovery that he was
born the year of Maqoma's expulsion from the Ceded Territory.

In December 1850 another frontier war broke out. Loss of land and European penetration in a number of forms—military, missionary and even settlement—were the root causes of this, as of other frontier wars. As in 1846, Tiyo Soga declared himself in favour of the Colony. The gap between his world and traditional black society was even wider now. Yet he was still a black and in due course identified himself with their aspirations, especially solidarity in the face of white cultural and territorial encroachment.

Ordination

Driven from his school at Uniondale, Tiyo Soga fled, together with the other Caffrarian missionaries, to Grahamstown in the Colony. There Robert Niven, it seems, suggested that he return to Scotland and study for the ministry. Against the wishes of his father, and with financial assistance from an anonymous source, he sailed from Port Elizabeth in June 1851 in company with Niven.

On arrival in England Tiyo Soga was singularly impressed by the celebrations surrounding the erection of the Crystal Palace. Apparently this reinforced the desire within him to return home and civilize his fellow countrymen. Once in Glasgow he was among friends. The John Street Church congregation welcomed him; the Sunday School and Session undertook to pay for his education until he was ordained. Yet, in spite of this, there were those who, perhaps under the influence of incipient racism, lifted eyebrows at 'one of the barbarians who have been fighting against us' now attending Glasgow University.

During his years at Glasgow Tiyo Soga read copiously in the works of historians, theologians and other intellectuals such as Prescott, Macaulay, Boswell and John Bunyan. *The Pilgrim's Progress* was a 'constant companion during his academic career'—perhaps he identified himself with Pilgrim. He attended Arts classes at Glasgow University during the winter, Hall in Edinburgh during the autumn and every second month he appeared before the Presbytery of Glasgow for examination in theology and for preaching practice. He was well thought of by friends and mentors alike as a modest, hard-working young man. As a result of the 1850 frontier war, increased attention was focussed on the blacks, and he found himself in constant demand as 'a real Kaffir—a countryman of the world-famous Makomo', as his biographer John Aitken Chalmers put it.

16 Tiyo Soga

On 23 December 1856, at the John Street Church, Tiyo Soga was ordained a minister of the United Presbyterian Church. Two weeks earlier he had received his licence to preach. After his ordination he was invited to preach at various congregations and other religious gatherings. This he did at considerable physical and consequently mental cost, as he was already suffering from tuberculosis. The disease was endemic in his family, and was ultimately the cause of his death. During the next fifteen years of his life he suffered recurring bouts of ill health, which generated morbid introspection.

But he was, withal, of optimistic disposition, as shown by his cheerful approach to what he called *'the horrors of matrimony'*. On 27 February 1857, he married Janet Burnside, a pretty Scots girl. She was a faithful companion to him during the difficult years ahead, and a devoted mother.

Once he had completed his studies, Tiyo Soga sailed for South

17 Janet, Tiyo Soga's wife

Africa on 13 April 1857. He was never to return to Scotland again; but it had bequeathed to him the riches of western culture. This made him appreciative and loyal to Scotland, and it also made him sensitive to the 'plight' of his fellow countrymen who, according to his westernized outlook, needed to be civilized, and through civilization converted to Christianity. At this stage in his career he was, in company with his fellow white missionaries, critical about what they conceived to be the grosser aspects of black society. However, his views about this changed during the next decade, under the influence of continuous colonial prejudice on the one hand, and territorial pressure on the other.

Colonial prejudice against blacks and, indeed, against mixed marriages was clearly evident on arrival at Port Elizabeth, where a black man with a white woman leaning on his arm virtually stopped the traffic, to the cry of 'Shame on Scotland!'. Nevertheless, Tiyo Soga was well received when he preached to a packed congregation in the Wesleyan church in Port Elizabeth and, later, at Trinity Church in Grahamstown. This was certainly partly due to the novelty of a black minister. On the other hand, Tiyo Soga quickly established an enviable reputation as a preacher (especially in the Xhosa language) which grew over the years. The Xhosa, Mfengu and Khoi to whom he preached on his way to British Kaffraria displayed as much amazement at a black minister as did the colonists, but it was the white reaction which cut deepest.

Mgwali

On reaching British Kaffraria, the Sogas settled at Mgwali mission station, some forty miles from King William's Town, where Tiyo served the United Presbyterian Church until 1868. The land around Mgwali had been depopulated by the cattle killing of 1856—7. A Xhosa prophetess, Nongqause, and her uncle had communed with the spirits of the chiefs who had commanded that the people destroy their cattle and corn; thereafter, it was promised, the whites would be swept into the sea and the cattle and corn restored. But there were no miracles and the population of British Kaffraria was reduced from 105,000 to 37,000. The cattle killing had been a protest against white encroachment, material and spiritual, but it weakened the blacks in the face of further colonial pressure, as well as opening the way for increased missionary activity. Tiyo Soga saw a divine purpose in the catastrophe: all in all, he observed, 'the prospects of all missions in Kaffirland were never better. We have now nothing to fear from wars.'

Tiyo Soga was deeply conscious of the reluctance of traditional black society to change its way in the face of Christianity and civilization; 'heathen customs and practices' were strong. Missions had successfully established themselves in Kaffraria, but efforts at propagating the Gospel were resisted by the core of Xhosa society. However, on the fringes of that society the missionaries were more successful, winning converts among the outcasts, the halt and lame, and among the Gqunukhwebe, who did not enjoy the same degree of social cohesion as the Xhosa. There was concerted opposition against all mission stations by the chiefs and their *amapakati* (counsellors). They distrusted the missionaries as alleged agents of the colonial government and they also feared their preaching which aimed at the abolition of rites and customs which provided the cement of society on which the authority of the chiefs rested. Tiyo Soga was lumped together with his white missionary brethren as an enemy of Xhosa society.

Yet, at Mgwali, in spite of adversity, Tiyo Soga established outstations for preaching, and schools where native agents were active. Some four to five hundred men, women and children lived on the station, many of whom were Mfengu.

In 1860 Mgwali enjoyed a visit from Prince Alfred (later Duke of Edinburgh). The royal party, accompanied by the Governor of the Cape Colony, Sir George Grey, passed from Port Elizabeth overland to Durban. Soga gave an address of welcome and, together with Sandile, Ngqika's successor, and Charles Brownlee, the Ngqika Commissioner, was invited to accompany the prince to Cape Town. They first touched at Durban to collect the royal party and on arrival at Cape Town Prince Alfred presented Tiyo Soga with a magnificent Bible. Soga was deeply touched. Two years later the Prince died and Soga mourned his passing as though he were a close friend. This deep attachment to royalty stemmed back to when as a schoolboy he had walked from Glasgow to Dumbarton to catch a glimpse of the Queen. Tiyo Soga was always loyal to authority, even colonial authority, which he saw as a means of disseminating Christianity and civilization among the blacks. This subservience to authority, so noticeable in his negotiations with government about the establishment of the mission station at Mgwali, was partly attributable to his Calvinist background.

Yet he was not narrowly sectarian, and preached generously at a variety of churches whenever he visited the colony. There were, however, other reasons for these visits. By the mid-sixties he was a sick man, and his tuberculosis was aggravated by his damp and uncomfortable house at Mgwali. In 1862 he was 'thoroughly prostrated' at King William's Town, and passed through a crisis of confidence in himself and his work. The following year he undertook a recuperative journey to Basutoland (Lesotho), but in 1865 he was once again forced to take a furlough of six months in Cape Town. These were troublesome times for Tiyo Soga as his second son, crippled by infantile paralysis, gave him much cause for concern. The progress of the Gospel at Mgwali was dishearteningly slow, which accounted for his cautious evaluation of missionary achievements before the Cape Native Affairs Commission of 1865.

Yet there were positive achievements. In 1866 Tiyo Soga completed the translation into Xhosa of the first part of *The Pilgrim's Progress*, published by Lovedale under the title *Uhambo Lomhambi*, which has now became a classic. He also continued writing Xhosa hymns, and by the mid-sixties was collaborating with his missionary brethren in producing a Xhosa hymn book which contained ten of his original hymns. It was published in 1873 under the title *Incwadi yamaculos okervungwa, yezikolos zika Krister, ezisemaxiseni* ('A book of hymns to be sung in Christian schools'). In 1868, when Tiyo Soga moved to Tutura, the first moves were made towards a revision of the Xhosa Bible, which consisted of a conglomeration of texts by a number of missionaries from various societies, including the Wesleyan and Berlin Missions. A Board of Revisers of the Kafir Bible was constituted and Tiyo Soga was the natural choice as the representative of the United Presbyterian Church Mission. The Board began work in 1869 on the four gospels, but Soga died before they were printed in Xhosa.

According to John Chalmers, his biographer, he also collected 'Kafir fables, legends and proverbs, fragments of Kafir history, rugged utterances of native bards, the ancient habits and customs of his countrymen, and the genealogy of Kafir chiefs with striking incidents of their lives.' Much of this is lost, but some fragments appear in the articles which Tiyo Soga wrote regularly for *Indaba* (published by Lovedale). Between 1862 and 1871 he contributed eight articles on subjects relating to the blacks (mainly the Xhosa), in which he discussed matters of a moral, didactic and even 'national' kind, ranging from 'Loans and Debts', and 'Christians and Chiefs' to 'A National Newspaper'.

Thus Tiyo Soga's writing was not narrowly religious but embraced social, economic and political matters. Certainly his most important piece of writing, from the perspective of black nationalism of the twentieth century, lies buried in the *King William's Town Gazette and Kaffrarian Banner* of 11 May 1865. It is entitled, 'What is the Destiny of the Kaffir Race?' Written under the pseudonym 'Defensor', it is the first published statement of black consciousness in the history of South Africa.

The circumstances surrounding the publication of this remarkable article involved John Chalmers who published an article of the same title in *Indaba* in February 1865 which appeared in the *King William's Town Gazette* on 3 April. Disillusioned by many years of unsuccessful struggle in propagating the Gospel and 'up-lifting' the blacks, Chalmers stated bluntly that 'Either this people are to rise in the scale of civilization, and play an important part in the history of this colony, or else every year must witness their extinction until at last they pass away, and be forgotten forever.' In March of the same year it was rumoured that the colonial government was contemplating the removal of the Ngqika beyond the Kei river. The plan fizzled out, but the feeling of insecurity it generated was infectious. On 10 March 1865, Tiyo Soga recorded his apprehension about the removal, which could only lead to difficulties—to say the least. Thus when Chalmers' *Indaba* article was reprinted in the *King William's Town Gazette* on 3 April, he once again recorded his disquiet in his private journal (25 April) and then sent the 'Defensor' letter to the *Gazette*. This letter is thus identified through his journal entry. Both the journal and the letter question the assumptions of the steady degeneration of the black race and its incapacity for improvement. However, the journal entry is the more graphic, full of raw emotion:

> *The Bible is the only Book whose predictions to me is law—Africa God has given to Ham and all his descendants—My firm believe [sic] is—that nothing shall ever dispossess them of this inheritance—that God will keep the Kafir in his Southern portion of it— and that God will so overrule events as always to secure this.*

Thus Tiyo Soga justified black territorial integrity on the basis of the Bible; he also emphasized the size of Africa and the huge numbers of its black inhabitants. Divinely ordained by God to people the continent, the blacks were tenacious, durable and thrived in adversity. This is the first evidence of *Africa-consciousness* in the history of black thought, and it is Tiyo Soga's unique contribution to the origins of black nationalism. Already in 1865, writing in *Indaba*, Tiyo Soga had conceived of a Ngqika 'people' or 'nation', a constituent part of the wider 'family of the Kaffir tribe'. This 'people' had certain 'national' attributes which included hospitality, the art of conversation, a sense of humour and a weakness for exaggeration. He had no objection to western civilization, which enlightened the mind, but expressed concern for its lesser benefits, such as intoxicating liquor, which corrupted the blacks. His ideal black society was one which was purged of obnoxious rites and customs by Christianity. Certainly western civilization would press heavily on the blacks, but wearing European clothes did not mean subservience to the whites. As he put it, 'This "Morning Sir" of the Xhosa people whenever they see a white face is very annoying.'

Basically, Tiyo Soga believed that God had created all men equal, but that 'education, civilization and the blessings of Christianity' had made differences between them. Soga had an unshakable faith in the integrity of the blacks, who possessed all the elements out of which 'a noble race might be made'. Above all, it was Tiyo Soga's belief in his own negritude (the refining of black consciousness into a positive doctrine) which made him so confident about the capacity of his people to lift their heads high. The Reverend Robert Johnston, who knew Soga well from Mgwali days, noted that

> *Tiyo Soga had an honest pride in his manhood as a* pure *Kafir. He was disposed to glory in his Kafirhood. He did not bow down before anyone, because of his own black face. . . . Hence he was not disposed to demean himself, when treated slightingly or shabbily, by a fearful or slavish submission. He seemed at such times to grow taller before you, as if he would say, 'I am also a man! a gentleman! a Christian!'*

The intensity of Tiyo Soga's negritude is evident in the advice which he gave his children when they left to be educated overseas:

> *You will ever cherish the memory of your mother as that of an up-right, conscientious, thrifty, Christian Scotchwoman. You will ever be thankful for your connection by this tie to the white race. But if you wish to gain credit for yourselves—if you do not wish to feel the taunt of men, which you sometimes may well feel—take* your place *in the world as* coloured, *not as* white *men; as Kafirs, not as Englishmen. . . . For your own sakes never appear ashamed that your father was a Kafir, and that you inherit some African blood. It is every whit as good and as pure as that which flows in the veins of my fairer brethren.*

He was immensely proud that he was descended from a 'long line of powerful, eloquent, independent councillors', and that among his own people he was 'a Kafir of the Kafirs'.

Thus during the sixties Tiyo Soga emerged as the unacclaimed precursor of black nationalism. He is the South African counterpart of James Africanus Horton, James 'Holy' Johnson and Edward Wilmot Blyden in West Africa. There is no evidence

that he was influenced by them; his thoughts and solutions seem
to be uniquely his own.

Tutura

This crystallization of thought took place mainly at Mgwali,
from where he moved to Tutura in 1868. Tiyo Soga had long
felt that there should be a mission station among the remnants
of the Gcaleka. Sarili, the Paramount of the Xhosa and chief of
the Gcaleka, had been driven from his lands in what is today the
Kentani-Willowvale area of the Transkei, across the Mbashe.
Early in 1864 he was allowed to return with the remnants of his
people to a segment of their former territory east of the Kei.
Sarili was in a weak position and hence asked Charles Brownlee, the Ngqika Commissioner, for a missionary. Chiefs sought
missionaries for a variety of reasons ranging from diplomatic
advantage to the benefits of irrigation—the desire for Christianity was low on the list of priorities. Tiyo Soga, who understood Sarili well, attributed political motives to the move. In
July 1865, Soga and Bryce Ross, of the Free Church of Scotland,
visited Sarili. The proposed mission to the Gcaleka was
delayed because of Soga's illness but in 1868, with the usual help
of fellow missionaries, he settled in at Tutura.

There was no doubt that Sarili was resentful about having a
missionary at all. Like other chiefs before him, he saw missionaries as the precursors of dispossession; and he was doubly
sensitive because all but a third of his country had been given to
Mfengu and Thembu: thus Tiyo Soga gloomily predicted that
even though the Gcaleka did not oppose the establishment of
the mission they would now, more than ever, 'resist the introduction of the Gospel'.

The lot of missionaries in Xhosaland was certainly not an
easy one. They were poised between God and mammon, and
a wrong move diplomatically could result in dire consequences. There were occasions when Tiyo Soga found himself
dragged into the political vortex of frontier affairs. In
1868 he supported the Ngqika when at a great meeting they
asked that Charles Brownlee be retained as Ngqika Commissioner. But the request was refused by the colonial government. Equally, in 1870, he saved the life of one Maki, a
counsellor of Sarili, who had fallen foul of the Paramount,
by advising him to flee. This particular incident plunged
Tiyo Soga into gloom about the future of his countrymen, for

the reason why Maki had been singled out by Sarili was that he belonged to a small enlightened group who supported the mission and, according to Soga's journal, 'His people chiefly filled the house of God on the Lord's day, and impressions were visibly made among them.'

It was because of such limited success by the missionaries, coupled with an increase of missions and outstations, that a powerful anti-Christian sentiment existed in the sixties and early seventies, among the Xhosa in particular, just as strongly as in the thirties. Nativism, in the form of a reversion to heathenism, had reared its head at Mgwali in 1863, where the Ngqika Commissioner had to be called in to control the white-painted *abakweta* (youths undergoing initiation ceremonies). These youths were, apparently, supported by the elders of the church. It was clear that this was an attempt by nominal Christians, still loyal to the chiefs, to pillory a black, uncircumcised Christian missionary. It was but part of a widespread reaction in Kaffraria against missions. Tutura was no different. Even before moving there Tiyo Soga described it as a place 'where midnight darkness covers the people', and the incident involving the hapless Maki seemed to confirm this. Small wonder that from time to time Tiyo Soga was plunged into the depths of gloom. On one occasion, at Mgwali in 1862, he went as far as to privately confess to John Cumming that he 'sometimes had great regrets that I ever went to Scotland and entered the ministry'. Yet Tiyo Soga still persevered, expanding the mission where he could, with the help of his faithful native agents, some of whom had been with him for many years.

Tiyo Soga had a strong sense of duty, not only to his work, but also to his family. In 1863 Janet Soga took her second son, John Henderson, to Scotland to seek a cure for a paralysed limb. In Tiyo's own words: 'Parental duty and anxiety were intensified by the thought that the boy, now so happy and healthy, might grow up into a helpless man, and reflect upon his parents that they had not done more for his enfeebled limb. On such considerations, we must sent him home.'

The word 'home' was significant; Tiyo Soga put his trust in Scotland. (And at Mgwali today the older generation still expresses its admiration for that country.) In 1870 he sent his three eldest boys, William Anderson (twelve), John Henderson (ten), and Richard Allen (eight), there for their education. This he did to spare them the indignities which would have been heaped upon them in the colonial schools because they were coloured children. By 1870 the colour-consciousness of South African society had eaten deeply into Tiyo Soga's soul, and he had become, as Chalmers noted, 'over-sensitive about his colour and his nationality'.

In June 1871, Tiyo Soga set out from Tutura to establish a new outstation. He was caught in a cold, misty drizzle which is so characteristic of winter in the Transkei. Trapped for several days in a damp hut, he returned to Tutura a sick man, and died on 12 August 1871. The funeral was attended by many of his fellow missionaries, including John Aitken Chalmers, who later wrote his biography, published in 1877.

Janet Soga stayed on at Mgwali with four of the children. Nearby lived Tiyo Soga's mother in her declining years. Old Soga also outlived his son, dying in 1878, in the last of the frontier wars. Tiyo Soga had hoped that his children would follow him and devote themselves to missionary work. His expectations were fulfilled by three of them. Of his four sons the eldest, William Anderson Soga, studied medicine at the University of Glasgow and later became a medical missionary in the Transkei, founding Miller Mission at Elliotdale. The second son, John Henderson Soga, also studied in Scotland and became a missionary in the Transkei, founding the Mbonda Mission in Griqualand East. He was the author of several books, including *The South-Eastern Bantu*, and he translated *The Pilgrim's Progress, Part II*. Of Soga's three daughters, the second engaged in mission work in the Transkei.

Tiyo Soga's death aroused great interest in the colonial press—the *Grahamstown Journal* noted: '[T]his was a new thing under the South African sun! A thieving Kaffir, a marauding Kaffir, the irreclaimable Kaffir, a University-educated missionary of the Cross!' There was also a reassessment of values on the part of some: 'Men cannot despise the Kaffir race, as they contemplate it in him.' Yet Tiyo Soga could not compete against the overwhelming force of two hundred years of history which had generated deep colour-consciousness among the whites of the Colony. He was socially accepted only by missionary, church and upper government circles. Even his own people were suspicious of him. He was thus a man of two worlds, who ultimately decided to throw in his lot with the blacks. It is significant that his last days were spent looking towards the Ngqika homeland where he had spent his youth.

His Two Worlds
Tiyo Soga was a committed Christian and, therefore, could not accept many aspects of black society which were an affront to Victorian morality. Western civilization, of the proper sort, was the solution; through civilization the blacks would be improved and thus facilitate the acceptance of Christianity. This could be attained with the help of the colonial government. Yet there was the rub—God, who had created all men equal, had situated the blacks in Africa which He had designated as their continent, and the whites were an alien intrusion into it. In the ultimate analysis, Tiyo Soga wanted to maintain black territorial and cultural integrity. Black institutions which were not inconsistent with Christianity should be maintained wherever possible. This would give cohesion and security, the foundation stones of black dignity, which was a source of strength in the face of alien cultural pressures associated with conquest. Yet within himself he was a divided man, with the call of black society jostling with his admiration for the seductive wider world beyond. Tiyo Soga never found the solution to his own difficulties. He lived on a territorial and psychological frontier which partly accepted the western educated Christian black as much as it did the white missionaries. But on the frontier, black pagan Africa lay on the one side, and white Christian society on the other, and both were uncompromising in their rejection of an alien presence. This is probably why he had a streak of melancholia in him. The Reverend Robert Johnston observed that

> *A tone of sadness pervaded his whole missionary life. It was impossible to get at the cause, and yet, perhaps, it was the fact that he stood* alone. *His social position, as an educated man, made him tower above his race, yet he must have felt that there remained an unbridged gulf between himself and the white race.*

In opting for the blacks (yet clinging to the benefits of western civilization) Tiyo Soga developed a strain of exclusiveness which is discernable in black nationalism today. He called upon people of colour to assist one another, to patronize each other's businesses and shops. He contributed to the origins of nativist (separatist) churches by frequently using the great hymn of Ntsikana, thus giving black congregations ethnic cohesion and emotional strength. His philosophy of black consciousness and negritude was only partly revealed to a limited audience reading *Indaba* and, later, Chalmers's biography. These thoughts have lain quiescent for a century. His hymns, on the other hand, were, and are, an integral part of black, Christian worship. In the Mgwali church there is a plaque to his memory, reminding one that he was the first ordained minister, a devoted Christian missionary, a scholar, an attentive father and 'an Ardent Patriot'.

NOTE

Soga's journal is in the Howard Pim Library, University of Fort Hare, South Africa.

FURTHER READING

Donovan Williams, *Umfundisi: A Biography of Tiyo Soga, 1829–71* (Lovedale, forthcoming).

John Aitken Chalmers, *Tiyo Soga; A Page of South African Mission Work* (1st ed., Edinburgh and London, 1877; 2nd edn., Edinburgh and London, 1878).

H. T. Cousins, *Tiyo Soga, the Model Kafir Missionary* (London, 1897).

H. T. Cousins, *From Kaffir Kraal to Pulpit, the Story of Tiyo Soga, First Ordained Preacher of the Kaffir Race* (London, 1899).

J. Henderson Soga, *The South-Eastern Bantu* (Johannesburg, 1930).

9
John Tengo Jabavu
1859—1921

An Mfengu, the son of Christian converts, John Tengo
Jabavu became teacher, preacher, newspaper correspond-
ent and political agent. It was, however, as editor of
Imvo Zabantsundu, which he founded in 1884, that he
was best known in the late nineteenth-century Cape.
Errors of judgement and changing circumstances much
reduced his influence in his latter years.

One of the effects of the wars of the *Mfecane* was to uproot
several traditional states in the area of Natal and Zululand,
sending the inhabitants fleeing over the Drakensberg mountains into the highveld or southwards along the coast to seek
refuge. Such rootless communities proved to be fertile ground
for evangelization by Christian missionaries and westernizing by
agents of European societies. They became nurseries for the
production of the new elite of the colonial period, when conquest and colonization had made the traditional elite virtually
ineffectual and irrelevant. This essay traces the emergence of a
modern leader among the Xhosa-speaking peoples in the Cape
Colony.

John Tengo Jabavu was of Mfengu origins. His ancestors were
among those who were led out of Gcalekaland in May 1835 by
the Cape colonial government, and settled near Fort Peddie in
the Ciskei. Although they had been well received by Hintsa and
his Gcaleka people, the Mfengu, probably because of their subordinate status in Gcaleka society, the pressure of a growing
population on a limited land area and missionary instigation,
became restive and seized the opportunity of the Sixth Frontier
War to rebel against the Gcaleka and emigrate from Gcalekaland. The land on which they settled near Fort Peddie soon
proved insufficient for their rapidly increasing numbers, and
they became dispersed in many districts of the Eastern Cape.

18 Jabavu

In the Seventh Frontier War (War of the Axe) the Mfengu again fought on the colonial side and as a reward were given land in the upper portion of the newly annexed district of Victoria East and in the Fort Beaufort district. Mfengu families that had been in the service of farmers since 1836 now returned to the new settlement near Fort Beaufort.

The Reverend John Ayliff of the Wesleyan Mission started a mission station at Healdtown in 1853 and the parents of John Tengo Jabavu were among the Mfengu converts who came to live on mission grounds there. John Tengo was born on 1 January 1859 at the village of Tyatyora near Healdtown and received his primary education at the mission school. In 1875 on completion of his training as an elementary school teacher, he took up a teaching post (at the tender age of seventeen) at Somerset East. There he combined the duties of schoolmaster and lay-preacher for the local Methodist congregation. His activities as a lay preacher to the Somerset East congregation marked the beginning of a life-long career of active and devoted work in the service of that church.

Tengo Jabavu's teaching spell at Somerset East also paved the way for his distinguished career as a journalist. It was while employed as a teacher that he began to regularly contribute articles to several English newspapers, including the *Cape Argus*, whose renowned editor Saul Solomon became his friend and hero. He also apprenticed himself to the office of the printer of the local newspaper in Somerset East, a move suggesting he may already have been planning a journalistic career. The exchange copies at the newspaper office provided him with a valuable source of information on the politics of the country. At the same time they contributed towards his ideas about race relations and the politics connected with them. He paid particular attention to verbatim reports of debates in the Cape House of Assembly, and from then on he closely followed the ramifications of Cape politics in particular, and maintained a lively interest in political issues in general.

Isigidimi and Lovedale

While teaching at Somerset East he received private tuition from Professor Thomas Kyd of Gill College for the Matriculation examination of the University of the Cape of Good Hope, and made rapid progress in Greek and Latin. Meanwhile his contributions to the *Cape Argus* and other newspapers led Dr James Stewart, the famous missionary and principal of Lovedale College to invite him to edit the Lovedale Xhosa journal *Isigidimi Sama-Xosa* ('The Xhosa Messenger'). Tengo Jabavu took up that position in 1881.

Tengo Jabavu's contract was for three years. During the nineteenth century Lovedale was among the foremost educational establishments for both blacks and whites in South Africa. Jabavu found its environment tremendously inspiring, and enjoyed the intellectual and cultural environment. Among Tengo Jabavu's contemporaries at Lovedale were S. P. Sihlali, Elijah Makiwane, Isaac Wauchope, Mpambani J. Mzimba and John Knox Bokwe. Jabavu threw himself into the intellectual life of the institution, playing a key role in its debating and literary society, as well as studying and giving instruction to elementary classes in Xhosa and Latin. In 1883 he passed the examinations for the Matriculation Certificate—the second African to accomplish that feat.

Under Jabavu's editorship *Isigidimi* 'gained fresh life and vigour' but it also began changing in character and in tone.[1] Jabavu used the missionary journal to make political comment. This became more pronounced after 1883 when he became the principal African agent and canvasser for Mr (later Sir) James Rose Innes, who was contesting the parliamentary constituency of Victoria East. This brought him into conflict with Dr Stewart and almost certainly accounted for his departure from Lovedale at the end of the contract. Confronted with the choice of continuing at Lovedale and suppressing his views; returning to the teaching profession with its restricted scope for his talents; or striking out on an independent career, he courageously chose the third alternative. After briefly trying his hand at farming in the Peddie district and toying with the idea of studying law, he turned to journalism.

His apprenticeship at Lovedale opened Jabavu's eyes to the need for an organ to express the point of view of the black people of the Cape Colony. There were thousands of African voters but there was no political journal to direct their thinking and interpret issues for them. There were many more potential voters who required to be educated about their political rights. Until the founding of his own paper the only newspapers run for Africans were missionary organs, concerned with promoting literacy and Christianity. The reluctance of missionary journals to accept articles of a political nature meant that Africans who desired to express themselves on current political issues had to use the columns of the white English press. Under the direction of Saul Solomon the *Cape Argus* had been popular with many African writers. After 1881 when that paper was more under the influence of Cecil Rhodes, its policy tended to be one of 'prudence' in racial matters, in deference to the interests of the great mining industry with which it became more closely involved. This meant that political critics and commentators no longer had unrestricted access to its columns.

Imvo Zabantsundu

Although Tengo Jabavu had a detailed and clearly worked out plan for a newspaper, he lacked capital. In 1884, however, he was assisted by two white liberal friends, Richard W. Rose Innes and James W. Weir, both of King William's Town. They guaranteed the necessary capital and arranged a printing contract with the *Cape Mercury*. On Monday 3 November 1884 the first issue of *Imvo Zabantsundu* ('African Opinion') came off the printing press.

With the appearance of *Imvo* Jabavu was in possession of an unique instrument for influencing black political thought and action. The first issue of *Imvo* showed that he was not unaware of this tremendous responsibility. He observed that for over a century missionary labours among Africans had bred a large 'class' that had learnt to loathe the institutions of barbarism and to press for the better institutions of a 'civilized life'. But this group of 'reclaimed' Africans was separated from their less fortunate kinsmen of the 'heathen' state. *Imvo*, accordingly, hoped to perform the function of 'a rope to tow those stragglers to the desired shore'. The same issue of *Imvo* pledged itself, in analysing politics, to follow principles rather than men.

Between 1884 and 1890 Jabavu used his newspaper as a most effective weapon to hit at segregatory legislation, to expose politicians or political groups whose attitudes towards Africans were motivated by feelings or ideas of racism, as well as to speak generally on behalf of the down-trodden and other victims of injustice. An example of the battle waged by Jabavu on behalf of the voiceless was the support and prominence *Imvo* gave to the case of the King William's Town pastor, the Reverend Davidson Don, who denounced a Burghersdorp Boer for killing a black servant. Jabavu also fought the cases of several other victims of oppression—among others was Chief Mbovane Mabandla of Tyhume, who was being unjustly cheated of his hereditary rights by a vengeful white District Commissioner with the connivance of the Cape government authorities; and the Reverend R. N. Mashaba of the Methodist Church in Mozambique, who was persecuted by the Portuguese administration of that territory.[2] By drawing public attention to the plight of individuals or groups of individuals Jabavu helped to exert pressure on those who had responsibility.

His voluntary assumption of spokesman for groups in distress made many Africans, especially those in the Cape Colony, look to Jabavu and his paper as their mouthpiece. *Imvo* was founded at the height of the Thembuland Trek controversy, when some two hundred frontier farmers, many of whom had assisted in quelling the Thembu rebellion of 1880–1, suddenly moved in and occupied an area from which several African groups had been expelled. These illegal squatters had the support of Jan Hofmeyr (Onze Jan) and the Afrikaner Bond. Hofmeyr maintained that by occupying the vacant land the Boer squatters were doing the Cape Colony a service, namely, ensuring that the 'tribes' expelled would not be able to reoccupy their former home district. In a series of editorial articles Tengo Jabavu severely criticized the Cape government for encouraging what he termed 'progressive dispossession of the Natives'. Because of the threat of land alienation in the Glen Grey district, he encouraged the Thembu and other groups to abandon the traditional communal land tenure and have their holdings surveyed and titled. He believed that individual land ownership would protect the lands of many Africans from being encroached upon by white farmers or being appropriated by the government.

Jabavu had another reason for encouraging individual land tenure—this was the only form of tenure recognized as valid for purposes of qualifying for the franchise. Jabavu had always recognized the importance of the vote for Africans in the Cape Colony, and aware that Africans could no longer influence the direction of politics through armed conflict, he saw the solution in substantial participation by Africans in Cape politics through the ballot box. For the last two decades of the nineteenth century, especially the decade beginning in 1881, the validity of his analysis could hardly be gainsaid. Thereafter European assault on the position of the black voter, plus the steady deterioration of the economic position of the blackman in the Cape Colony, made over-reliance on the vote as a weapon, and belief in the merit of representation of black interests by white politicians in a white parliament, distinctly chimerical.

From the time of the founding of *Imvo*, Jabavu used it extensively to organize the African vote in the Cape. He eloquently discussed the advantages of being a registered voter, the qualifications required and the steps to be taken in order to be placed on the register. He announced the dates, times and venues of registration courts at which objections to black voters' registrations would be heard, and helped Africans to arrange for legal representation at such sessions. In addition Jabavu watched the voters' lists and promptly exposed any irregularities in these, especially the exclusion of Africans qualified to be on them.

In addition to the influence he wielded through his paper, Jabavu employed the many contacts he had with white liberal (both Cape and British) politicians to obtain some amelioration of the political difficulties of Africans and to try to get them more chance of participation in the political system of the Colony. At the time there were three distinct political groups in the Cape parliament. There was a group of conservative English-speaking members drawn principally from the frontier districts of the Cape, comprising mainly descendants of 1820 settlers and led by J. Gordon Sprigg. This group tended to be both anti-African and anti-Afrikaner in outlook. Another influential group was the one that developed into the Afrikaner Bond, led by Hofmeyr, which tended to be sympathetic to the northern Boer republics, as well as anti-African in orientation. The third group was smaller and its supporters came mainly from the more settled and commercialized English-speaking communities in the cities. The prominent spokesmen of this group were men of professedly liberal views, James Rose Innes, John X. Merriman and J. W. Sauer. Jabavu supported the members of this group, whom he often referred to as 'the friends of the natives'.

The support which this liberal group gave to Jabavu's strenuous campaign against Sprigg's Parliamentary Registration Bill of 1887 appeared to justify his choice of political allies of the African voters. Jabavu dubbed the measure the 'Native Disfranchisement Bill' and argued that it was designed 'to muzzle the Natives'.[3] Despite the strong opposition to the Bill it was passed and as the Parliamentary Registration Act it resulted in

30,000 African voters being taken off the register.

In 1892 Cecil Rhodes introduced another measure designed to emasculate the Cape black vote. The Franchise and Ballot Bill also met with determined opposition from Jabavu, though many observers did not fail to notice the rather muted tone of his denunciation of this particular bill. This was because his closest political allies—Rose Innes, Merriman and Sauer—were members of the Rhodes ministry that was responsible for the Franchise and Ballot Bill. Thus although Jabavu opposed the Bill, his criticism of it weakened in tone and he began looking for redeeming features in this monstrous piece of racist legislation. His attempt to find some reasonable explanation and merit for the stand of 'the friends of the Natives' eventually affected adversely his stature as champion of black people's rights.

When Rhodes introduced the Glen Grey Bill in 1894, ostensibly to give Africans a permanent tenure based on individual ownership, Jabavu again opposed the measure. He correctly pointed out that what the Bill gave with one hand it took away with the other. Rhodes' Glen Grey Bill came much too late. Africans had been so dispossessed that the principle of 'one man one lot' had become an unrealizable dream. Jabavu discerned the underlying motives of the measure—namely, to launch a frontal attack on the African vote by disqualifying all registered voters who held their lands under the communal land tenure system, and to tax Africans so as to compel them to go and work as labourers at the mines or other places of work run by Europeans. Thus although he personally favoured individual land tenure Jabavu was correct when he concluded that the Glen Grey Bill embraced 'a multiplicity of objectionable principles', while the few that seemed favourable were so clogged with official checks and counterchecks as to be absolutely valueless to Africans.

In his paper Jabavu took a strong stand against pass and location laws, and continued a sustained attack on pass laws until the end of 1889. While no new pass laws were enacted in the Cape Colony between 1889 and the formation of Union, some of the objects of pass laws were achieved through location and labour laws. Jabavu maintained that such legislation was absolutely unnecessary; and if it could be justified at all then the laws should be applied to all persons in the Cape Colony regardless of race.

Jabavu raised no objection to Africans leaving their residential areas to go and work for Europeans. Generally he encouraged Africans who were economically hard pressed to go out and work, but he bitterly attacked their exploitation by unscrupulous employers, whose tactics he exposed in *Imvo*. He frowned on the importation of labourers from countries outside South Africa, and urged government to tap South Africa's own labour resources first. He suspected that behind most of the attempts to import labour lay a desire to reduce wages at the mines and other labour intensive public works or industries. He argued that the country would derive much benefit from utilizing more of its own African labour. According to him, this would increase the purchasing power of Africans, and lead to a general rise in revenue.

It was to be expected that his personal experiences would make educational achievement rank high among his goals for Africans of the Cape Colony, and in *Imvo* he gave much praise, encouragement and publicity to all efforts to improve or expand African education. Jabavu used his newspaper to express the aspirations of Africans in the field of education, stressing the need for greater efforts in providing industrial and agricultural education, and training of African teachers qualified to give instruction in such areas, as well as the adequate endowment of the schools themselves. But unlike some whites, he opposed the notion that there were certain types of education not suitable for the African pupil. He argued that many Africans who had been educated side by side with whites had become important leaders of their communities. Without underrating the positive contribution of missionaries, he urged greater state participation in African education.

His greatest efforts in African education were in connection with the founding of a college of higher learning at Fort Hare. This campaign he waged intermittently, with others, from about 1908 until the college opened in 1916.[4] He tackled the task of organizing support for the college with such singleness of purpose that many came to speak of that institution as 'I. Koleji ka-Jabavu' (Jabavu's College). He sat on its first Governing Council and remained a member until his death, while his son, Mr (later Professor) D. D. T. Jabavu, was one of the first two lecturers appointed to the staff of the College of Fort Hare.

Challenges and Loss of Influence

Tengo Jabavu's efforts on behalf of Fort Hare College did much
to redeem his image as a leader of the black people in the Cape
and to a lesser extent in South Africa. Before this there had been
a progressive decline in his stature as a spokesman and representative of the African people. For fourteen years since the
founding of his paper Jabavu's strivings on behalf of his people
had made him the foremost leader not only in the Cape Colony
but throughout the whole of South Africa. However, in 1898
another black newspaper was started in East London by the
Reverend Walter Rubusana and other members of the Cape
African elite who were in disagreement with Jabavu's strategy
in politics. *Izwi Labantu* ('The Voice of the People'), was founded
as a counterpoise to *Imvo Zabantsundu*; the dissatisfaction of
many Cape Africans with the role played by Jabavu in Cape
politics especially during the 1890s gave urgency to the need for
a rival organ.

One of the results of the Jameson Raid was the disintegration
of the group of liberal independents led by Rose Innes, Merriman
and Sauer. Jabavu first worked in close cooperation with Rose
Innes and the Colonial League, while Merriman and Sauer
gravitated closer to Hofmeyr's Afrikaner Bond. Disagreement
over the selection of candidates for the general election of 1898
made Jabavu transfer his support from Rose Innes and the
League to Merriman and Sauer, who were already working very
closely with the Afrikaner Bond. Then in March 1898 Hofmeyr
made a pre-election speech in which he claimed he had been
unjustly represented as the enemy of the African people's political liberties. Jabavu seized upon this 'epoch-making address' to
give his full support to the Bond coalition with the erstwhile
'friends of the Natives'.

The stand taken by Jabavu during the general election of 1898
cost him the confidence of many African followers who turned
away because of his association with the Bond. Then came the
South African war of 1899–1902. As the outbreak of the conflict
between Boer and Briton became imminent, many Africans
perceived in the approaching strife an opportunity for blacks to
rise and fight for their freedom. Jabavu started by counselling
neutrality on the part of Africans along the lines ordered by
British officials in South Africa. As the war progressed Jabavu's
paper became more and more critical of the war, for which he
blamed Milner, Rhodes and other members of the 'war party'.

This was in contrast with *Izwi Labantu* which, along with the Progressive Party, stood full-square behind Her Majesty's forces in the war against the Boer republics.

Tengo Jabavu's anti-war stand brought about the closure of his paper under Martial Law regulations in August 1901. The paper did not re-appear until 8 October 1902. The closure of *Imvo* was a further blow to Jabavu. It not only meant personal financial loss but his political fortunes also took a deep dive. During the time *Imvo* was silenced *Izwi Labantu* had been unchallenged in its criticism of Jabavu, not only on his war stand but also for his general ideas about Cape politics. By the time *Imvo* reappeared the damage to Tengo Jabavu's image had been done.

As if that were not bad enough, Jabavu committed a series of blunders that ultimately neutralized the limited recovery his reputation had made as a result of his work for Fort Hare College. His handling of the question of Union lacked consistency. One moment he would sharply criticize the exclusion of Africans from the deliberations that shaped the South African Union; another he would sneer arrogantly at the expression of similar sentiments by other African leaders, maintaining that so long as there were men of the calibre of Sauer in the government blacks had no cause to be worried. Jabavu's isolation from other leaders was temporarily broken in 1909 when he joined a deputation of other black leaders which went to London to protest against the South Africa Act. In London he argued that the imperial government's sanction of the discriminatory draft South Africa Act set a precedent for more racist legislation.

Back in South Africa, he opposed Rubusana's decision to stand for election to the Cape Provincial Council in 1910, arguing that such a move would set Europeans more implacably against African rights. Notwithstanding, Rubusana was elected and became the first and last African member of a provincial parliament. When several black leaders planned a united front by forming themselves into the South African Native National Congress early in 1912 Jabavu was conspicuous by his absence. In 1911 he had attended the Universal Races Congress in London. On his return he held aloof from plans to found the South African Native National Congress and instead formed his own organization, the South African Races Congress. Likewise, when the newly formed Congress attacked the Natives Land Act of 1913 *Imvo* was the only organ that saw any merit in it. Clearly Jabavu was now blindly following Sauer.

Tengo Jabavu's crowning folly was his decision to stand against Rubusana in the constituency of Thembuland during the Provincial Council election of 1914. By creating a three-cornered contest he divided the African vote and facilitated the election of the European candidate, A. B. Payne. Thereafter Tengo Jabavu had virtually no influence left as a political leader. In 1920 he became a member of a native education commission. Throughout his adult life he maintained a very close association with the Methodist Church. He served that church as lay preacher circuit steward and became one of the first and longest serving African lay members of the South African Methodist Conference. In 1879 he had been one of the founding members and first Treasurer of the Native Educational Association. For some time he was a member of the King William's Town Municipal Council representing the ward of Breidbach. He died on 10 September 1921 while attending a meeting of the Governing Committee of Wesley House at Fort Hare.

His Significance

There can be little doubt that for some time Tengo Jabavu through his newspaper *Imvo* made himself the undisputed champion of African political rights. However, he concentrated his energies in organizing and directing the small group of black voters in the Cape Colony, whose strength never rose above ten per cent of the entire Cape voting population. Also his emphasis on African participation in the white-ordained politics of the Cape Colony severely limited his tactics, since these were of necessity conditioned by the vagaries of white politics. His concern with participatory politics ultimately overshadowed his efforts to speak on behalf of different groups of Africans all over South Africa, and made it difficult for him to acquire the stature of a national, rather than a mere provincial, leader. In this respect, however, he did not differ radically from other political leaders of his time such as M. K. Gandhi, A. Abdurahman or J. H. Hofmeyr, who could all be said to be striving for sectional rather than national interests.

Tengo Jabavu's conservatism made him readily accept the white man's categorization of the African population into two elements, 'civilized' and 'uncivilized', and the unjust corollary flowing from it—namely that only the 'civilized' Africans deserved the same political rights enjoyed by whites. Because of his acceptance of these doubtful premises Jabavu saw the solution to the problem of African rights as lying at the Africans' own door. Africans should strive hard to uplift themselves and thereby convince whites of their suitability to enjoy the same political rights as the whites themselves. On the other hand liberal whites such as 'the friends of the natives' would create the bridge for acceptance on equal terms of 'civilized' blacks. Jabavu accordingly hesitated to adopt a strategy that would amount to 'rocking the boat' which might frighten potential white sympathizers. His tactics were based on practical realism rather than ideological conviction.

One of the criticisms usually levelled against Jabavu was his apparent inability to form a lasting political organization, except for ephemeral and *ad hoc* expedients formed to deal with specific crises as they arose. This was probably due to his fear of being eclipsed by younger and more militant leaders, who were showing signs of being impatient with his personal contacts or backstairs approach in politics. Yet although Jabavu never succeeded in establishing an organization that could develop into a national movement, he deserves credit for being the first African leader to mount a sustained campaign to arouse political awareness among the Africans of the Cape Colony, and demonstrate practically the role that could be played by the press. However, his inability to co-operate with other African leaders prevented him collaborating with the founders of the South African Native National Congress and, thereby, throwing his considerable weight and talents behind that organization.

Tengo Jabavu's efforts, therefore, fall outside the context of nationalism. But he was the fore-runner of the nationalist movement among the blacks in South Africa. He was the pioneer politician whose work prepared the way for the more spectacular achievements of later African leaders. Subsequent leaders such as Pixley Seme and Clements Kadalie, who succeeded in founding more stable organizations, can be said to have sown in ground that had been tilled by Tengo Jabavu.

In the final analysis the failure of Tengo Jabavu as a political leader was the failure of liberalism in Cape politics. Not only were there powerful forces opposed to the growth of liberalism, but even the professed liberals were not striving too hard for an unqualified open society at the Cape or in South Africa. To most of the white liberals, Africans like Jabavu were setting their sights too high. Whereas to Jabavu the Cape Constitution Ordinance with its colour-blind franchise symbolized the possibility of the opening up of a brave new world of political equality for all civilized men, most of his white friends considered that goal unattainable. They were not prepared to go the full distance towards its realization.

Although Tengo Jabavu's importance in the history of political development of Africans in South Africa is generally admitted, when account is taken of the opportunities he had for organizing the Africans, it appears that his failures were more striking than his successes. Many will accordingly remember him not for what he did, but for what he could not do.

NOTES

[1] *The Christian Express*, 1 November 1920; Bokwe Letterbook, South African Library: J. Knox Bokwe to R. W. Rose Innes, 6 July 1885.

[2] *Imvo Zabantsundu*, 27 January and 18 July 1905.

[3] *Imvo Zabantsundu*, 13 March 1887.

[4] M. O. M. Seboni, 'The South African Native College, Fort Hare, 1903–1954', D.Ed. thesis, University of South Africa, 1959.

FURTHER READING

D. D. T. Jabavu, *The Life of John Tengo Jabavu* (Lovedale, 1923).

E. Roux, *Time Longer Than Rope* (London, 1948, 2nd edn., Madison, 1966).

L. D. Ngcongco, 'Jabavu and the Anglo-Boer War', *Kleio*, II, 2 (October, 1970).

L. D. Ngcongco, 'Imvo Zabantsundu and Cape "Native" Policy 1884–1902', M. A. thesis, University of South Africa, 1974.

H. M. Wright, ed., *Sir James Rose Innes: Selected Correspondence (1884–1902)* (Cape Town, 1975).

Index

160